DUE PROCESS DENIED:
The Detained - The Families - The Fallout

Cynthia Hughes

with contributions from Sean Morgan, Geri Perna, and Genevive Spencer

BOMBARDIER
BOOKS

Published by Bombardier Books
An Imprint of Post Hill Press

ISBN: 978-1-63758-941-0
ISBN (eBook): 978-1-63758-942-7

Due Process Denied:
The Detained – The Families – The Fallout
© 2023 by Cynthia Hughes
All Rights Reserved

Interior Design by Yoni Limor
Cover Concept by Genevive Spencer

Designations used by companies to distinguish their products are often claimed as trademarks. All brand names and product names used in this book and on its cover are trade names, service marks, trademarks and registered trademarks of their respective owners. The publishers and the book are not associated with any product or vendor mentioned in this book. None of the companies referenced within the book have endorsed the book.

All Scripture quotations, unless otherwise indicated, are taken from the Holy Bible, New International Version®, NIV®. Copyright ©1973, 1978, 1984, 2011 by Biblica, Inc.™ Used by permission of Zondervan. All rights reserved worldwide. www.zondervan.com The "NIV" and "New International Version" are trademarks registered in the United States Patent and Trademark Office by Biblica, Inc.™

This is a work of nonfiction. All people, locations, events, and situation are portrayed to the best of the author's memory.

No part of this book may be reproduced, stored in a retrieval system, or transmitted by any means without the written permission of the author and publisher.

BOMBARDIER
  BOOKS
Post Hill Press
New York • Nashville
posthillpress.com

Published in the United States of America
1 2 3 4 5 6 7 8 9 10

To the J6ers, may you and your families be whole again very soon. May you never be discouraged to fight for what you believe in when this is all over.

Mom, Dad, and Angel Boy, you are forever missed. Dad, I hope you are proud. Angel Boy, please always watch over your dad.

My husband, the Love of My Life. My knight in shining armor. You rescued me and saved my life. You showed me hope when I had none left. You are all my dreams come true, and I could not have done this without your love and support. Thank you for always choosing me.

My babies. Thank you for your support, your encouragement, and your understanding while I pursue JUSTICE. Please never forget to always follow your heart and fight for what you believe in.

Brother, I love you.

MB (sheesh), thank you for encouraging me to Jump.

CONTENTS

Foreword 7
Tim's Statement 11
Who Is Cynthia Hughes? 13
January 6 19
Tim 29
Due Process Denied 43
The Jails 51
The Families 63
Patriot Freedom Project 85
Matthew Perna 95
Trump #45 113
Help—Action—Resource 119
Acknowledgments 123
About the Author 131

Miss Erica, thank you for helping to make this book a reality. I am grateful for your help in this.

A special thank you to the contributors who assisted with co-writing and editing. Your contribution to this book will help further the important work of the Patriot Freedom Project's efforts in helping and aiding the January 6 defendants and their families. The support of this effort is so important to bring truth to light and help bring aid in this humanitarian crisis.

A heartfelt thank you goes out to:
G
Sean Morgan
Geri Perna
Ed Martin

This book would not have been possible without each of your contributions. Forever Grateful to all of you.

With love,
Cynthia

FOREWORD

Standing in the cemetery looking up at the slitted windows of the jail.

I said, "Can they see us?"

Cynthia Hughes took a deep breath.

"I'm not sure. I hope so. But you know, it matters more that we're trying. We're here."

"We're here." There might be no better phrase to capture the spirit of Cynthia Hughes and her fight to help the prisoners of January 6 and their families. It's not a matter of success in court or in the prison or even in the homes of the families…because sometimes it seems successes come few and far between. But it's more about being faithful to the call. Being present for these people.

From the moment I met Cynthia Hughes—on a phone call and later in person—I recognized someone who was on a mission. The mission was not of her own choosing, nor for her own advancement. The mission was to help her family and to help others.

Cynthia's days are filled with phone calls from families, visits with elected officials and policymakers, and planning for fundraising and distribution of funds. Oh yes, she also must talk with lots of lawyers and find out if they're serious about the work and if they're worthy of support. (This might be her least favorite part of the effort—too many lawyers!)

She's also emerged as a public voice, which she uses regularly and loudly. It's helped shine a light on what's wrong in the prisons and courts *and* has helped bring around public opinion. Using her voice has also earned her attacks by the press and rotten grifters. On social media and in other ways, she's discovered that the worst of America will focus on the good people like her. It's ugly, and apart from a few Jersey-style rants, she takes it all with dignity and turns their hate into energy for her good cause.

One more aspect of Cynthia's work is important to mention. Like any good leader, she attracts people of great talent and energy. These men and women are willing—for reasons that many of us cannot easily explain—to give their time, talent, and treasure for the good cause. It's an amazing movement.

What started as a grassroots effort has become a movement based within the Patriot Freedom Project. With professional communications, legal analysis, advocacy, and service to the prisoners and their families, PFP is a force multiplier.

I've watched Cynthia meet with famous journalists, senators, representatives, and other big shots and media and culture; she's fearless. And when she met with Donald Trump, she carried the day and charmed the President. They were kindred spirits, and he recognized her as a doer, not just a talker. When these people meet with Cynthia, they see a woman who is not in it for the politics or the game, but for the right reasons. She is in it for the people.

America is great because of so many things that we take for granted, like our Constitution and our founding values.

But most of all, we are great because of *we the people* and the families we live with and whom we love. Cynthia Hughes is the best of America. She loves her husband and her children, but that love Cynthia has for her family and for America is real and palpable and it extends to her neighbor and to all of us. When you read these pages or are so blessed and get to spend time with Cynthia Hughes and see her work hard for the Patriot Freedom Project's efforts, you will know how special this is.

It's a gift for the J6 prisoners, for their families, and for America.

—**Ed Martin**, President of the Eagle Forum Education & Legal Defense Fund
Washington, DC
October 23, 2022

TIM'S STATEMENT

January 6 produced false narratives for our crooked government and press, allowing an unprecedented political inquisition and flagrant abuses of constitutional rights. In a world of so-called "Christian MAGA constitutional conservative patriots" (in truth gatekeepers, grifters, clout-chasers, and controlled opposition), it took a God-fearing New Jersey housewife to get actual help to January 6 defendants and their families. Seeing the results of her efforts first-hand and watching the unceasing attacks on her, I think Cindy qualifies for sainthood. She has exemplified the Beatitudes better than any other figure connected to this struggle. Cindy was my only lifeline while imprisoned. Patriot Freedom Project has helped the persecuted and entrapped, and its critics are typically those in favor of the persecution and entrapment that has destroyed so many lives. I've lived with the men whose families have been helped for the better part of two years. The envy and malice of copycats and saboteurs have not and will not stop this good work—work which must continue until the liberty of our people is restored.

—**Timothy L. Hale**
BOP #25995-509, formerly D.C. DOC #376441

WHO IS CYNTHIA HUGHES?

At the time of this writing, over nine hundred American citizens have been accused of crimes in relation to January 6. When the targeting first occurred, it was pure chaos; the FBI was raiding the homes of families and detaining defendants. The defendants were thrown into solitary confinement for months with only one hour per day to call families and lawyers. This was excused because of "COVID."

Because everything happened so fast, there were no coordinated responses from conservatives and lawyers, or from anyone at all for that matter. There needed to be a strategy to handle the gargantuan task at hand, to support these enduring people. These families with limited finances, connections, and legal knowledge had to defend themselves against their own government, which clearly has unlimited resources and the full backing of the corporate media and tech machine. As if that wasn't enough, the families had to survive without their loved ones (and their incomes), and there was no person or organization willing to step up to help or support them.

Beyond the financial and legal help that was so desperately needed by these families, there were deep-rooted emotional needs that were being left unmet. Many of the defendants who were harassed by activists and the media have spouses who were forced to deal with the collateral damage from these egregious acts, and they desperately needed a community to fall back on; community is so important during times of struggle.

This is the chaos that Cynthia Hughes was thrown into when she decided to help her honorary nephew Timothy Hale.

Tim's public defender was a Trump hater, and Cynthia went into action to try to give Tim a shred of hope for justice.

Cynthia didn't have to help Tim. She had her own biological kids to care for. But as I have gotten to know Cynthia, I realize that when you gain her loyalty, she will fight fiercely on your behalf as if you are her own blood.

Cynthia didn't stop at just helping Tim get a world-class Judge Advocate General (JAG) lawyer appointed to him. She took everything she learned and passed it on to other J6 families.

She could have stopped there. She could have given some tips and said, "Good luck." But in the face of the overwhelming odds stacked against her, she decided to "stand up" for an "untouchable" group of people.

Cynthia saw a need and decided to do something about it. When she saw hundreds of detainees and family members in need of legal advice, financial support, and community, she didn't just say to herself, "I'm not a lawyer, I'm not rich, and I'm not a social worker." She must have believed that her God was bigger than these problems laid before her. And she must have felt a lot of love and empathy for all those people to take the further actions she did.

Some people don't have that empathy gene. They have a stone-cold wall built around them and the people they view as outsiders.

But Cynthia has some special genes. Ones that allow her to feel others' pain and consider mere strangers to be family. I think that's why Cynthia can imagine each detainee being her own son…or nephew.

And perhaps as a survivor of her previous marriage to a criminal (who was sometimes in jail), she can relate to the wives of J6 detainees who have been left behind to support families on their own.

When people first meet Cynthia, they probably think to themselves, *Here is a very normal person from New Jersey.* Cynthia does a phenomenal job of making people believe that she is simple, but just because she doesn't tout herself as an intellectual doesn't mean she isn't extraordinary. Anyone who takes on the responsibility of caring for hundreds of families is most definitely a hero.

Cynthia didn't just have the faith to do that, she also had the skill to bring the right people together to make it happen, to battle institutions with multibillion-dollar budgets like big tech and big media. A nice lady from New Jersey turned out to be their worst nightmare. It turns out that tenacity and heart are a lot more important than sophistication and connections. However, she will be the first to tell you that she isn't doing it alone. She has a knack of getting a lot of favors from God. I think she is as tenacious with her prayers as she is with her actions in the material world.

Her nephew Tim was the one who supplied her with the names and contacts of the initial family members to start a support group. It was a young priest on an internship who showed her that you can help save someone's life if you keep on "showing up" with love.

Cynthia overcame a life of heartbreak and abuse. She went from victim to victor. Now she's paying it forward. Whatever dream she has today is overshadowed by what she conceives is next.

As a friend looking at her life from the outside, I just can't believe what she believes she can do…what she keeps setting out to do. There have been a lot of roadblocks and naysayers along the way. Literal naysayers who just say "no" to everything she wants to accomplish. But this Jersey girl doesn't take "no" for an answer.

She deals with the arrows of the enemy all the time. Sometimes she has a good cry about that. But then the next moment, she picks up her phone and gets a text from another J6er who "just needs to talk to someone." Instead of saying, "That's not my problem," she insists, "This is the mission I signed up for."

I think that's why God keeps helping her with miracles. She volunteered to do this, and she keeps the faith…so God keeps supplying her with what she needs to complete this mission.

Cynthia has said that the January 6 problem isn't going away. This will be a journey of many years to advocate for families who have been damaged and broken. But in the face of those future years in the trenches, Cynthia gets up with excitement, because for every setback there is ground gained. For every detractor, there is a donor to the cause. And for every enemy, there is an ally.

Despite the fact that Biden's Department of Justice continues to target and harass American protesters and dissenters, Cynthia knows she's a part of the greatest political movement of all time. Trump is on her side, and God is on her side. By the way, I'm on her side, and everyone who gets to know the sweetheart from New Jersey is on her side! She collects friends the way most people collect acquaintances.

    For Cynthia, friendship is not just a social connection. It's a loyalty oath. So, it doesn't matter if your name is Joe Biden or Merrick Garland. You don't mess with her friends. Or else. Or else…she might have to go into "prayer warrior" mode. So, you better watch out. When Cynthia's prayers go into action…they move mountains.

—**Sean Morgan**

JANUARY 6

January 6, 2021, was a day that changed America forever. It was a day most Americans will never forget, although many would probably love to be able to. On this monumental day in history, a sea of Trump supporters went to the nation's capital to hear their commander in chief speak. This was a day when some of the seventy-four million Americans who voted for Trump in the 2020 election would peacefully assemble to make their contempt for election fraud heard.

There were many questions about the 2020 election leading up to this day, and these questions remain unanswered as I write this entry over a year later. The climate of our country leading up to Election Day was one that has never been experienced before. The division Americans have been enduring these past few years because of these unanswered questions is at an all-time high and is ever-increasing.

The American people were fed up with political games, which is why they decided to stand in solidarity with their beloved president on January 6. Between the coronavirus, the lockdowns, the mail-in ballots, and now the black cloud lingering around the outcome of the 2020 election, Americans were faced with uncertainty, and this uncertainty showed at the ballot box. January 6 was a day for the American people to say, "Enough is enough." These people were no ordinary group of Americans; they were Trump's loyal base of support. They were "MAGA" manifested.

They hoped to change the outcome of the 2020 election. They went to the Capitol singing the country's anthem and marching proudly to protest the very questionable outcome of the 2020 election. Despite the anger, there was a great sense of joyful camaraderie.

Being honest, is there really any question that the election of 2020 had inconsistencies? Many would ask the question: "If this was such a rock-solid election and there was no chance of fraud, then why not provide evidence that will help the American voters who questioned the validity of this election feel confident in their vote?" As we listened to Joe Biden and Kamala Harris give a message of unity, their actions went on to tell a different story.

If eighty-one million people really voted for these two, then why not move mountains to help quell the division over this? Why not do whatever it would take to answer the lingering questions that remain? Instead of uniting Americans the Democrats fanned the flames of chaos.

Over the course of Donald Trump's four years in office, the country became incredibly divided. There were two types of people: those who loved Donald J. Trump and those who hated him. I've always believed that more people than not think Donald Trump is a great president, but many are too afraid of cancel culture and retaliation to speak up and share their true opinion. In his four years in office, this man suffered from relentless attacks. Nothing he did was right according to those who had such disdain for him. He, as well as his family, was under constant scrutiny. Even though he had a legion of loyal supporters, those who opposed him were not going to allow him to serve as president for another four years. They wanted him out at any cost, even if it meant destroying our country and countless lives in the process.

After four years of constant bashing of a president that so many loved, Americans grew increasingly frustrated with being silenced on what they chose to support and believe in. The blatant disregard for this president angered many. In 2020, the country watched the news every day in horror as they witnessed actual riots that lasted months. People were tired of the double standards and of the hypocrisy around the lack of outrage over the real violence.

There is no question that supporters were disgusted with the barrage of attacks on their president and his supporters. As Election Day grew closer, President Trump's rallies drew thousands of people, each rally surpassing the last. Trumpers would line up for days to see and hear their president speak. He was loved by so many, and still is. By the time we got to Election Day, there was really no question about who would be the winner of the 2020 presidential election.

As election night progressed, it was becoming evident that the forty-fifth president of the United States would have another term, but then something happened. Some might say that something very sinister was going on. How could one win the states of Texas, Florida, and Ohio; pick up sixteen Republican seats; and then proceed to lose the presidency? It would seem to many, especially to Trump's loyal supporters, that this was impossible. However, on November 7, 2020, Joe Biden was declared the next president of the United States!

Some Americans felt cheated; some felt disbelief or perhaps a mix of both. Were we not watching blatant election inconsistencies? The questions raised included the covered-up windows at polling stations around the country, no Republican challengers being allowed to observe Election Day operations and the counting of votes. A Trump campaign director in 2020 stated that he was receiving calls and texts that Republican poll watchers were being kept far away from counting tables in Philadelphia. We all watched the many suitcases being pulled from underneath tables filled with ballots in Georgia, and let's not forget the poll worker from New Jersey who admitted to discarding mail including election ballots. This man would later plead guilty to one count of mail desertion.

Was the election really stolen? How could this be? As we watched in the days to come, it became quite clear that something was going on. It seemed every judge, court, and person to hear any argument from Trump's camp would not even entertain the idea of election fraud, even if the proof was placed right in front of them.

This left many Americans feeling a bit hopeless. How could you trust your government if they were only entertaining one side of the argument? Why would our very own chief justice of the Supreme Court want to see so much pain in our country? It would seem to our new president and vice president that allowing the division to grow was worth it if it meant keeping Donald Trump out of the White House. The words and more importantly the actions of the new president and vice president showed this country they just didn't care about the people.

Look at what we have witnessed regarding Hunter Biden. Why are Trump's children attacked repeatedly over "made-up" allegations, but we are watching videos of Joe Biden's kid smoking crack and talking about issues of corruption the Biden family is accused of? Have you seen the interviews with Tony Bobolinski? He vows that the country will be shocked at what an actual probe and investigation of the Biden family will uncover. Even with these stark contrasts in action, those who despise Trump would rather remain silent.

Something seemed amiss with this election, and it was all that was being talked about by Trump and his supporters. What would come next would bring so much heartache to this great country. On December 19, 2020, President Trump tweeted to his supporters that there would be a big protest at the Capitol: "Be There, Will Be Wild!" he tweeted. As expected, #45's loyal supporters showed up to express their love and regard for him. How could anyone predict the trap that would be waiting for them? And how could anyone deny the enormity of the crowd in support of Trump? Why doesn't this matter to those we elected? Trump's real supporters were used as bait on January 6, and there is no denying this!

Now let's be honest, Trump is and always has been a president of law and order, a president who does not support violence. I have seen evidence that many bad actors, more specifically crisis actors, were brought in to create the chaos that would become "the January 6 riot." This was a well-planned attempt to trap Trump and keep him from running in 2024! I often say that the Trump Hater Club did Trump supporters a big favor.

As I write this in October 2022, I believe Trump will announce he is running even if Merrick Garland and the Biden DOJ attempt to slap him with the ridiculous charge of obstruction, along with anything else that they can throw at him and pray will stick. But they will have given this country six years of TRUMP: two years of campaigning and rallies from 2022–2024 and then four years of a second Trump presidency with most likely the best female running mate. A great big thank-you should be given to the Trump Hater Club!

It seems those who were voted into office decided once they were in that they no longer needed or wanted to listen to the concerns of the American people. The RINOs decided to not hear what their constituents were saying. It's quite sad to see the power trips and blatant disregard for the hardworking American voter. It seems as if our vote did not matter to our elected officials.

While peaceful and patriotic Trumpers were listening to his speech while singing and waving their flags, there was something brewing just steps away at the Capitol that would forever change the lives of many American people. As the MAGA crowd of Trumpers marched on the Capitol, they arrived upon a sea of unrest. There was already rioting and disruption happening, and many have said that when they arrived at the Capitol, there were people engaging in acts of violence who were not Trump supporters. If they weren't Trump supporters, then who were they?

As people gathered around the Capitol, many within the crowd became agitated. Was it purposeful, planned, or maybe even a staged event? According to eyewitness accounts by several of those charged for their role in the Capitol protest, the unrest that was already underway caused many to feel the need to act. They attempted to defend themselves against the police or agitators. Why would so many feel as if they had to defend themselves against our very own police?

Seniors lying bloody on the ground, young children there with their parents for this historic moment were sprayed with gas, and many were locked in a heated exchange with the police. People caught in massive crowds of hysteria were unable to move or turn around, so moving forward seemed to be the only way to get away from the violence, only to then be trapped.

Trumpers thought their fellow supporters were being harmed. Flash-bangs were being thrown into the crowd, and streams of gas were being sprayed from hoses. What was happening? Why were the police attacking Trump supporters? This is when things became very complicated. Nobody wants to see our great police officers (who swear an oath to serve and protect their people) be harmed, assaulted, or even lose their lives. Nobody wants to believe that our police would want to harm those they swore to serve and protect. So, what was going on? How could so many people commit such heinous acts against the police like this, and why would the police viciously and savagely beat Trump supporters with clubs, spray them with nerve spray, and throw flash-bangs at people's heads? These actions caused difficulties in hearing and seeing, further disorienting the crowd and creating more pandemonium.

There were flash-bangs being thrown, causing some in the crowd to be seriously hurt, people's hair to catch on fire, and many to collapse in pain. What a disheartening picture to imagine for those of us who were not present that fateful day. I recall watching this unfold on live television and thinking they wanted to kill the president or at least harm him. Some individuals who were present had been seen at other rallies, such as Antifa rallies, where they were noted to advocate for violence. This is evidence that something sinister was afoot.

Will we ever really know the truth of what happened on January 6? Could there have been other violent groups put in place to create a scene of anarchy, just to set up Donald J. Trump and his supporters? It certainly looks that way. Multiple people who were present that day have some explaining to do.

Why has the famous character Ray Epps, who was caught on tape telling Trump supporters to enter the Capitol, never been charged for inciting violence that day? Why were so many police officers just standing around while others were fighting to protect themselves from being attacked? Why were the doors to the Capitol opened? Why were known Antifa members seen inside there but never charged with entering and remaining in a restricted building (like countless others have)?

Why were filming permits taken out weeks in advance? Why were there so many film and video crews conveniently placed in certain areas inside the Capitol if the building was to be off limits that day to the public? How could two pipe bombs have been placed at both the RNC and DNC headquarters without anybody knowing about them (after what was described as a "thorough sweep" was performed before Kamala Harris arrived at the DNC at 11: 30 a.m.)? How did Nancy Pelosi's daughter know what would become of that day? Nancy Pelosi's daughter literally had a documentary film crew with her at the Capitol on January 6. Why was Nancy Pelosi being filmed that day by her daughter? What was Nancy preparing for that needed a documentary film crew to follow her around the Capitol on January 6? So many questions, and "we the people" deserve answers to all of them.

Prior to January 6, 2021, there had been two other "stop-the-steal" rallies. These rallies were different from the January 6 rally. At the earlier rallies, there were vendors selling drinks, porta-potties, open stores, and no curfews; but on January 6, it was very different. It was almost as if there was a desire for a riot.

Shortly before January 6, President Trump offered to properly secure the Capitol grounds, but in a January 5 letter DC Mayor Muriel Bowser rejected the president's offer. Why? Her response seemed so spiteful and intentional—almost as if the mayor, along with Nancy Pelosi and many others, wanted what happened on January 6 to occur. How could those who are elected to office be so obsessed with revenge and hate for the good of the American people? Why would the speaker of the House not have an interest in ALL voters of this country? So many Americans were overwhelmed with the frustration of their voices not being heard, their votes not mattering, and watching their president being bashed, belittled, and viciously attacked day after day. For Trump supporters, there would be no question that they would show up "front and center" for a president they so dearly loved.

On January 6 so much destruction occurred, many people were hurt, and several Trump supporters died. Will we ever know why things got so out of hand? There are many theories: bad actors, a preplanned attack, or a perfectly planned setup. Was it really so wrong to have questions about the legitimacy of the 2020 election? Why do Trump supporters have to face being canceled, attacked, and denied for speaking out about what they believed was a fraudulent election? Isn't this a free country? In the United States of America, we are supposed to be afforded the right to exercise free speech according to the First Amendment, aren't we? Why are Trump supporters punished for believing the 2020 election had some inconsistencies?

On January 6, thousands of Trump supporters went to the Capitol to exercise their right to peaceably assemble, only to be met with resistance from other "protesters," our very own police, and anyone who opposed Trump. The carnage of that day will not be forgotten. Furthermore, the aftermath of how January Sixers and their families were treated will remain a scar upon our country's history.

TIM

Oh Tim! It's not easy to write some of the things you'll read in this chapter about him. Where to begin? Timothy Louis Hale-Cusanelli was born in March 1990 into difficult circumstances—and that is putting it mildly!—to a young mother with many challenges and a father who was incarcerated when Tim entered this world. It can be agreed that he didn't have a great start in life. (Note: this is the only time I will use the name Cusanelli when referencing Tim; I will explain why later in this chapter.)

    It's not easy to explain Tim and his quirkiness, or some might say his odd personality, but please appease me as you read on while I do my best to explain this quirky, incredibly smart, insensitive, and sometimes bombastic jacka**. Tim would truly be in the fight for his life from the gates. I was present when Tim entered this world, and I held him when he was just minutes old. I knew we were in trouble when Tim was more curious about his new surroundings than he was about exercising his lungs. I held Tim for several minutes before he was whisked away to the nursery for his first medical inspection. I recall how alert he was, looking around at his new environment, hardly even a cry. As I did that motherly rock with Tim in my arms, I prayed silently as I knew he would be in for a rough time with the parents he was born to.

When I could, I tried to be close by as much as possible to provide some sense of security for Tim; it was important for him to know that someone would show up for him in his life when he was in need. Tim's mom and I are close in age. She was my very best friend most of my life, and we had babies at the same time. My firstborn was only a few months older than Tim. It wasn't long after Tim was born that his little life would start to spiral and he would be so burdened at such a young age. He lived with his mother for a short time after his birth before moving in with his paternal grandmother. From there, he went back to his mother, where he remained most of his life, but not without a lot of traumas.

Throughout Tim's teenage years, he had situations where he needed to come live with me at times. He always knew my door was open to him. Please let me be very clear: I love this kid as if he were truly my own son. As time would pass in Tim's little life, things became harder and harder for him. No child at such a young age should have experienced the burdens that Tim did. I tried to be the constant in Tim's life. Besides his great-grandparents, who were so wonderful to him and loved him dearly, he really had nobody else. It was important to me to be in his life; little children are not supposed to be burdened by grown-ups. I could relate to Tim; I knew what it was like to grow up in hard times as I too had a rough childhood.

I know all too well what it is like to be let down by the grown-ups. I wanted to save Tim from those adversities and shield him as best as I could. I needed this little guy to know he had someone who would always be rooting for him and in his corner; I wanted him to always know he had a place to turn to. A place of stability and security, which is something I have always been able to provide to him. Every kid deserves these things no matter what.

Unfortunately, life would happen, and there were times when Tim and I would be separated, which always broke my heart. I hate that at some of the most important times in Tim's life, I was not present. When I reflect on those times, it really pains me to think he had to face some very painful, and even happy, times alone. He experienced some very important rites of passage alone, and it just breaks my heart. I can't even begin to imagine what would have become of him these past twenty-one-plus months if I had not been in his life.

Tim has been failed so many times by the people he should have been able to depend on. At a young age, Tim was diagnosed as being on the spectrum. He is an incredibly bright person, and he knows history like nobody's business. This kid can tell you all about the Holy Bible from front to back without even opening the Good Book. His artistic abilities are profound, and his drawings and paintings are masterpieces. Tim knew what he wanted to become in his future—a history professor. Tim joined the Army Reserves after he was talked out of his desire to go active duty. Sadly, life simply had other plans for him. Tim had a lot on his plate during his school-aged years. He had to make sure the bills were paid and care for his mother. To do so, he worked two jobs and also had his commitment to the Army. This goes to show just how much responsibility he had on his shoulders at such a young age. This kid endured so much by the time he was seventeen, and it undoubtedly changed and shaped him in many ways.

Tim was closed off to those who wanted to extend a hand. He is incredibly independent and would never allow himself to be in debt to anyone. He has been burned so much by the grown-ups in his life and has been abandoned by not one but two fathers. Remember earlier in this chapter when I mentioned that you would only hear the name Cusanelli one time? Here's why. There was a time when Tim's mother tried to do right. She married a man who would become Tim's father in every sense of the word; he was good to Tim and adopted and gave Tim his name. The sad part is that he did all this only to abandon Tim when he no longer wanted to remain married to Tim's mother. He just left Tim after contributing a huge part to his upbringing and never looked back. How can someone be that cruel to a kid? I tried to reach out to him to tell him Tim needed his help, only for him to advise me never to contact him again!

Besides Tim seeing a doctor immediately upon his release from jail as a first priority, his second task will be dropping that name like a bad habit! How sad for this kid—everyone he thought he could depend on simply abandoned him. In my opinion, this was an ultimate letdown and betrayal for Tim. He had such a close relationship with this man, and just like that, he turned off any emotion he had about being Tim's father. As I said a few sentences back—Tim will drop that name like a bad habit when his life is once again intact! I will make sure of that!

Trust was not something that came easy to Tim, and I am sure by now you can see why. Tim's only escape became the Army. That is, until he discovered he could make people laugh. This is where it becomes touch-and-go with Tim Hale, and where it becomes hard to write about and defend him. What you will read next is in no way an excuse for Tim's questionable choice of words and some very insensitive "jokes," but everyone deserves the chance to explain. But first, let's talk about Tim's Army career.

Tim wanted to join the Army right out of high school, and he planned on going fully active. However, these dreams were put to a halt, only to be afflicted yet again (and with so much guilt) by his mother. He then ultimately decided to join the Reserves instead. Later in life, he would learn that was one of the biggest mistakes he would ever make. There were times in Tim's life when his mother and I were distant, and one of those times was during Tim's time in boot camp. There are two important pieces to Tim's life puzzle that break me every time I even think about them. One of those pieces is when Tim left for boot camp while his mother and I were on a hiatus from each other. When you join the military, during boot camp you take an official basic training portrait. What most may not know is that you must pay for this portrait. The day Tim went to take his portrait he had no money in the bank account he shared with one of his parents, and he could not pay for the picture. But graciously the photographer advised Tim that he could pay for these photos upon picking them up. Well guess what? This same parent burdened this eighteen-year-old kid yet again, and he would never pick up this very important photo. I am in tears as I write this entry; how could any parent do this to their own child? I am determined to track down this archived photo somehow! He deserves that picture—he earned it!

The second and equally painful heartbreak is when Tim graduated boot camp alone! It truly pains me to think of how let down and sad he must have felt.

How do we fix this for him? Can we even fix this for him? How does he heal from these betrayals? I hope over the course of time I have eased some of his pains and heartbreaks. I swore to Tim many years ago after a very serious and painful incident in his life that changed everything for him that I would never leave his side or be far from him again. I have kept that promise to him and only the Good Lord could make me break it. Many years ago, I was forced to decide whether to be the mother figure Tim needed or to continue the friendship with his mother. I chose Tim!

You should know that I have four children of my own, but Tim is also my child even though I did not birth him. It doesn't matter to him and me, because we love each other as a mother loves her son and a son loves his mom; I am the mother he knows. To say Tim has been to hell and back would be putting it mildly. Hiding from his pain was something that kept him going. Tim learned to hide his pain with offensive gestures or remarks of satire and protected expression.

Please know that I am in no way defending him for being an "a**hole" if I may be blunt. But being an a** doesn't mean you deserve to rot in jail for twenty months over your political opinions or hard-hearted choices in comedy. I assure you, there is more to Tim Hale than what the media has provided to you, and to those of you willing to take a chance on Tim and explore more of his unique personality, what you will discover is an eloquent and remarkable young man who has survived many odds. So now let me just get right down to it. Just some facts about Timothy Hale. Tim has no criminal history, at least not worth noting. He served honorably without any incident in the US Army Reserves for almost twelve years, until he was kicked out for participating in the January 6 protest despite the fact his charges had not yet been adjudicated. He was never charged with a violent crime for his participation in the J6 protest. Tim is nothing more than a shock jock, and I want to emphasize that he is an amateur comedian and satirist online, and no more controversial than comedian Bill Burr. His sense of humor focuses on tragedy and morbidity, with heavy usage of sarcasm and irony.

Much has been made by the prosecution of the contents of Tim's phone. These contents included offensive pictures, memes, and derogatory language. These are jokes for those with similarly edgy senses of humor. "Memes" are, by definition, internet jokes and satire, and may be repugnant to many people, but Tim's memes are not indicative of his alignment with white supremacism but rather his belief that tragedy is the basis of comedy. Tim considers himself an amateur comedian with his friends and on the internet, and his willingness to use slurs is no more alarming than many routines of modern comics. His persona combines the attributes of prominent figures such as Alex Jones and Sacha Baron Cohen's Borat character. Pictures and videos of Tim making offensive gestures or remarks are examples of satire and protected expression, not evidence of violent behavior or predispositions. Those stating "these jokes are not funny" ignore the reality that comedy is totally subjective (if people are laughing, it's funny to someone). Tim's offensive remarks are evidence only that he could be insensitive, which I assure you he is, but I also assure you more he is not a member of a dangerous ideology.

Tim has always vehemently denied that he is a racist or white supremacist. I have watched Tim grow and I have also watched him live a very hard and painful life, and if you knew what he endured, you would be cheering for him being the survivor he is. He has never made himself a victim of his circumstances and has always been hardworking. Tim loved serving his country and would give anyone the shirt off his back. He was the shop steward at his job over a group of diverse men. He proudly took this responsibility very seriously. He wrote letters to his congresspeople to exact change at the workplace being run by a woman who hates men. If Tim was getting himself a cup of coffee after working twelve hours straight, he got it for the entire crew. He is the guy who would work an overnight shift and then when his shift was over, he would go and get everyone breakfast sandwiches. He is the guy you can call in the middle of the night if your car breaks down, and the guy you can always depend on no matter what. All of this and more is true of Tim Hale.

There is much more to Tim than the overly insensitive pictures and memes that were released by this government and distributed by hateful media outlets from his private phone, which is where these images were meant to live indefinitely for his eyes only. This content does not define who Tim is or who he will be after this nightmare is over for him. Further, I do not condone Tim's choice of comedy; I have shared many times with him where I stand on it and his imperceptive judgment on his comedic choices. But the fact remains no matter how insensitive Tim is and is portrayed as, the truth cannot and should not be ignored!

The truth is, Tim went to the Capitol on January 6 after a long shift at work to support his commander in chief. He wanted to show his utmost respect for his president. In true Tim form, he wore a suit and tie along with his favorite hat to the Capitol. He arrived just in time to hear some of President Trump's speech. He did the patriotic walk toward the Capitol with many others. Tim describes those moments as happy. Everyone was talking, singing, skipping, and marching proudly. Upon his arrival at the Capitol, he saw people being harmed, and again in true Tim Hale form, he jumped into action to lend a helping hand. Tim helped many that day who were hurt and in pain. He was not charged with any violent crimes, and yet he has remained in jail for twenty months as of the time of this writing. He has bounced around between five different jails and eventually landed at DC Correctional Treatment Facility (CTF), marking the sixth jail where he has lived through more hell in his life. He will go to one more jail to serve his prison sentence and eventually a halfway house and finally home.

While in jail, Tim has eaten bologna sandwiches every single day for twenty months. If he is lucky, he gets a rotten apple with it. He doesn't see the sun, and he has lost hearing in both ears due to a horrible double-ear infection. While he was bleeding out of his ears with this infection, he received very little and poor medical attention; he never saw an actual doctor for this illness, and he suffered for many weeks, as it kept escalating without effective treatment. His mattress is one-inch thick, and he doesn't get religious services. Tim is Catholic and is the type of person who goes to church and reads his Bible religiously. By the time he goes to sentencing, he will have been deprived of this constitutional First Amendment right for more than twenty months, as he has had no access to any religious services.

Not only does Tim not receive religious services, but he also doesn't get any recreation time either. His character has been obliterated by the media, and yes more or less this is his fault because of his comedic taste, but be that as it may, Tim has been wrongfully detained for over one year for the books, words, and pictures he was in personal possession of. Isn't America supposed to be "the free world"? There is nothing free about Tim's circumstances.

Throughout this time, he has been denied his constitutional right of due process and was found guilty of a bogus felony charge. Who knows what he will face at his September sentencing? While yes, the public has every right to be disturbed over these awful pictures and allegations, I would like to think the public would be more concerned and outraged with the denial of due process to so many.

We live in the greatest country in the world, "the free world," and we literally have political imprisonment happening in this country. Tim has no criminal history, served his country, was not charged with a violent crime, and when he was asked to leave the building by the police, he did! Tim has spent twenty months locked in a cage denied many basic human rights, and sadly because of some dumb choices, he is not only being punished by the government and very biased media, but he is also being penalized by those who have the ability to help tell his story. Some in the media world are not any better than our very government when it comes to what they have done to Tim. I challenge those who have the fortitude and backbone to stand up and say I will defend Tim…but first I worry for him. What will become of him after this? He has lost his job, military career, and housing, but all of that will pale in comparison to the time in his life that he has lost.

During Tim's many status hearings and eventual trial, I listened to his judge and thought to myself often, How does this man live with himself; how does he go home at night and look at his own children knowing what he has done to Tim is wrong? This judge jailed Tim over words he said, history, books, and politics. After having a discussion with one of the people who came to understand Tim and care about what was happening to him, we realized when the DC jury read its verdict that there was nobody more thrilled than his judge. His judge now had the justification that jailing Tim was right and punishing him further was just.

Now his judge could relieve himself of the egregious act of jailing a nonviolent protester with no criminal history. That judge will have to live with the fact that he jailed a nonviolent protester because he simply did not like the politics of that person. Tim is the true definition of a political prisoner. I look forward to the day he can tell his story, for there is much to be told.

On the first day of Tim's trial, I knew he would never stand a chance with the selection of DC residents being vetted to sit on the jury. It was a three-ring circus, an absolute joke. These people loathed Donald J. Trump, and they were going to make sure Tim felt it. They were going to make #45 pay through my nephew, and you saw it on those who in fact were selected to sit on the jury. I watched DC resident after DC resident be asked how they felt about January 6. I listened as one after the other told the judge they were too emotional to sit on the jury, and yet this judge insisted these people had to do their civic duty. This blew me away, and I knew that Tim was going to be in some serious trouble.

Tim's trial should have never been heard in the city of DC. The prosecutor in Tim's case was the meanest person I have ever encountered; she was on a mission to destroy Tim's life. She couldn't accept that Tim felt the way he did about a president he loved and one he didn't. And because of their misalignment of views, Tim was going down. Her contempt for Tim was on full display for all to see. She was rude and disrespectful to not only the judge but to the defense team as well. Tim's judge allowed this charade the whole week. At one point this prosecutor released my private and personal information for all the media to see! She knew exactly what she was doing. These people are seriously disturbed.

I remember the moment that she asked her colleague to bring in the evidence. The evidence was the suit and tie Tim wore that day, and the full-size Trump flag Tim found on the ground inside the Capitol. Tim picked up the Trump flag and skipped around the Capitol even admiring the beautiful artwork of history displayed all around. I remember one of the government's witnesses being asked "What was Tim doing with the Trump flag?" and his answer, "DANCING!" It was a perfect answer and quite ridiculous. Tim didn't go in the staterooms or the chamber; he skipped around the crypt waiving his Trump flag, and for that he had to spend months in pretrial detention, enduring solitary confinement.

As I write this entry, he remains in solitary confinement. I hope by the time this book is released, Tim will be sitting here beside me writing his own book about January 6.

I don't know how Tim would have survived these last months without me, and I am grateful to God that he put me in Tim's life and that I was able to help him through this very dark time in his life. I am his voice out here beyond the walls of the system. What would have become of his personal effects? His books had already been lost once when his parent abruptly moved away without even a word to Tim and got rid of everything he owned, so I couldn't let something like this happen again. Can you imagine your parent doing such a thing to you while you were growing up?

When I finally got to speak to Tim after he was first arrested, I cried like a baby for him; I feared for him and his life. I didn't get to speak to Tim until the third day of his arrest. After hearing him assure me he would be OK, I made sure he knew his personal belongings would be safe and secure and waiting for him when he returned home. Glory to God I have been able to provide Tim a sense of peace in this; if he hadn't had that, this nightmare would have likely been beyond unmanageable for him.

On September 16, 2022, Tim will learn his fate, and he will be closer to getting his life back and picking up the pieces to start rebuilding from the ground up. I will be right by his side through it all to help him. January 6 does not define Tim! He will pick up the pieces and carry on in life, and I will make sure of that! Tim is going to be OK; he will land on his feet, as he always has, because he is built that way and really has no choice but to look up and ahead and persevere. Onward and upward, Tim.

Update: Tim was sentenced on September 22, 2022, to forty-eight months in federal prison. Can you imagine a man with no criminal history, at least not worth noting, who spent more than twenty months in solitary confinement conditions, served his country for more than twelve years, and committed no acts of violence on January 6, would be sentenced to such an egregious amount of time? Tim did not receive this sentence for his participation on January 6; he received this sentence because he had a judge who simply did not like him. Here is an excerpt of Tim's sentencing by the judge:

"I don't think the guidelines as calculated by me appropriately account for your racist and antisemitic motivation. I also believe the extensive damage and injuries caused on January 6th with 'your fellow rioters' require additional punishment beyond what my calculation allows."

Think about this for a second: regardless of how insensitive some things Tim has said are, he is protected by the First Amendment! Despite this judge stating he is not punishing Tim further for his rhetoric, he in fact did exactly that. Tim should be home right now and this judge knows it! This judge sentenced Tim over his rhetoric and for what other people did that day and it states just that in the judge's comments.

DUE PROCESS DENIED

What is due process? It is the fundamental right of any American jailed in this great country. The Fourteenth Amendment clearly states the following; "No State shall make or enforce any law which shall abridge the privileges or immunities of citizens of the United States; nor shall any State deprive any person of life, liberty, or property, without due process of law; nor deny to any person within its jurisdiction the equal protection of the law"—and yet here we are. There are more than ninety Americans and counting that remain behind bars because of their participation in the January 6 protest. This number is expected to grow, and I'm certain that it will by the time this book hits the stands. The majority of these people who remain behind bars were denied due process.

Some detainees have been tried and convicted and are awaiting their sentencing. Only a handful have started serving their sentences, but not before having their constitutional rights trampled on for many months. When these arrests started in January 2021, the defendants were being picked up from around the country and held in a county jail within their own jurisdiction. Most made bond in their state only to have their bond revoked by the DC courts before they even had the chance to be released. Prosecutors in these cases filed emergency orders in the DC jurisdiction that ultimately overturned the decisions made by judges in the defendants' home states. Once that happened, these defendants were moved to one of the jails that were housing J6 defendants. Moving from their home jurisdictions to the jail didn't happen overnight. These detainees were processed in multiple jails in varying states before they landed in the jail where they would languish for over a year.

Most people think that anyone arrested in connection with January 6 is immediately sent to DC or has been released, but this is not the case. These pretrial detainees are in different facilities around the country. DC is just one of the holding facilities, but there are others in Virginia, Pennsylvania, Florida, and Oklahoma. We even have one detainee, whom I call the Lone Wolf, being held in an ICE facility in Georgia. It's shameful that Biden's DOJ didn't allow these men and women to stay in their home states until their trial or a plea deal was reached. The damage that's been done to these families that have been separated for such a long time is irreversible.

Keeping the detainees in their home states until trial would have allowed the families to have access to see them. Being able to see your husband, wife, or parent is one of the greatest forms of support. During these traumatic times, these families needed support more than ever, yet they were forced to struggle on their own and were broken. Most of these men and women do not have a criminal history, and some have nonviolent charges like Tim.

Not only is it difficult for the families to see the detainees, but it's also nearly impossible for their attorneys to see them as well. Attorneys have quite literally been denied access to see the men and women behind bars and speak to them. When they do get to see their clients, it's usually in an open room which negates the attorney-client privilege. January 6 defendants have been denied their right to participate in their very own trial! This is unheard of and wrong, and this government knows it but they do not care!

These defendants would have likely received religious services had they been kept in their home states. Just another denial of the constitutional rights of these men and women. It has been very frustrating to sit back with my hands tied knowing I can't do anything. These Trump supporters who have been detained for more than one year and held in solitary confinement are political pawns for some of the politicians who just hate Trump so much that they will step on anyone to stop him from running for president again. During the summer of 2020, we watched in horror as cities were literally burned to the ground, police stations set on fire, Molotov cocktails launched at police vehicles, businesses looted, and theft happening on live television. The difference in the treatment of those who partook in truly violent riots versus the treatment of those who supported Donald Trump at the Capitol was night and day. The number of arrests and the consequences that those actual criminals endured for protesting for weeks on end are not comparable to the treatment of those who protested for a few hours on January 6.

And please let's not forget when the then vice president pick said on her social media platform on June 1, 2020, "If you are able to, chip in now to the MN Freedom Fund to help post bail for those protesting on the ground in Minnesota." The hypocrisy is truly so maddening! Imagine if Trump said this.

Let me share with you some insight into what the day-to-day life is like for the men and women who were denied the right to due process, as well as for their families. Those being detained in the district of DC like my nephew Tim have suffered the harshest conditions. The deputy warden Kathleen Landerkin has been accused of bias toward the January 6 detainees due to her hatred of President Donald Trump. Her behavior was caught on camera on November 3, 2021, when Deputy Landerkin denied entry to two US congresspeople, and this would not be the only time this deputy warden would deny our congresspeople entry to this jail. This deputy warden would lock the doors to keep out members of Congress who were visiting with the desire to do a wellness check on the January 6 detainees. Why would she deny a wellness check?

Eventually on November 4, 2021, Representatives Marjorie Taylor Greene (R-GA) and Louie Gohmert (R-TX) would be granted access to visit the men, along with their staffs. After their visits, Representative Greene wrote a comprehensive report of her findings. You can find her report at green.house.gov, and it is definitely worth the read. Representative Greene was able to confirm the many complaints coming out of DC CTF jail. During her appearance on Bannon's War Room, she recounted her visit to the jail the day before. She was alarmed by what she saw, describing some of the men dealing with serious medical issues. Although some men were moved after her report was released, sadly not much else has changed since then.

These guys are denied religious services: no clergy at all! Speaking for myself, I know during some of the hardest times in my life I needed my church, my Bible, and my priest so profoundly. We have had many clergies reach out and ask how they can help and provide services to these men. This jail, and I think most of the jails, is hard-pressed when it comes to giving certain life services to those incarcerated. This is something that should be looked at very hard with a fine-tooth comb. This nightmare has been very eye-opening, and there really needs to be a long, hard look at what is happening in the jail system. This is a conversation I plan to start really soon!

I recall the first phone call I received from Tim after he was arrested. He was exhausted, stressed, and worried, and all he wanted was his Bible. He asked if I could get it to him. I wasn't able to get his personal Bible to him, but I did get him a Bible immediately. While he was locked up in Essex County, New Jersey, waiting for his transfer to DC, we encountered a wonderful woman, whom I will leave nameless. She was an ombudsman for this facility and a warm, caring, and incredible light in those very dark days. She really helped me help Tim. She didn't care why he was in jail or what he was accused of. She said that wasn't her job; her job was to help where she could. She made a huge difference in Tim's time at that facility and took a lot of worry off me as well. May God always bless this wonderful woman; there should be more like her.

Due process should have provided these men and women with a fair and speedy trial. However, this fundamental right has clearly been denied. Not only were they guaranteed a fair and speedy trial as United States citizens, but they were also entitled to an unbiased judge and jury, which they definitely did not receive. Not a single January 6 trial should be heard in the city of DC, and every trial should be moved immediately! However, this is something that will likely never happen. This would apply to even those who are on home confinement.

To date, we have had multiple jury trials in the city of DC, all of which have resulted in guilty verdicts. Even bench trials are resulting in guilty verdicts. If you don't know what a bench trial is, it's when you forgo a jury and ask the judge to decide your guilt or innocence independently. Even with bench trials, nobody is receiving fairness in the city of DC, and again, every single one of these trials should be moved out of DC immediately.

Most of these judges are unable to separate their politics from their job. It's easy to recognize this when you pay attention to the remarks they make in the status hearings. Many of these judges despise Trump; therefore, anyone coming in front of them due to the January 6 protest doesn't stand a chance. During Tim's five-day trial, the bias and politics were on full display by the prosecution. During the argument by the prosecution, they brought in two examples of evidence. One piece of evidence was displayed quite flamboyantly when the prosecution dramatically opened a multi-foot-long box only to reveal a Trump flag! Don't you see the only person on trial is Trump?

These defendants are truly suffering and receiving the collateral damage of politics. They've been held in pretrial detention with their constitutional rights taken away from them, and as a result, have endured multiple status hearings where the federal Speedy Trial Act of 1974, which defined the speedy trial provision contained in the Sixth Amendment, was egregiously ignored by these judges. The Speedy Trial Act was enacted to prevent detained individuals from serving more unnecessary time than deserved, given the possibility that they are to be found not guilty. It would be unjust to have an individual who is not guilty serve time for a crime that they did not commit. The prosecution in all these cases has taken more than a year to turn over discovery, and some defendants at this very moment still do not have any (or all) of the discovery materials.

Essentially what this DOJ has done is to arrest people first and investigate them later. Many defendants were, and are going to, reject these outrageous plea deals. The prosecution asks to "toll" (pause) the speedy trial clock because they know they will get the jail time they request for these defendants, one way or another. Tolling the speed trial clock is important as it is supposed to provide instruction and rules in federal cases, such as the time between an indictment and trial. However, in these J6 cases, guidelines on the Speedy Trial Act are nonexistent.

Due process denial doesn't just affect the men and women arrested, charged, and indicted in these cases. Due process denial affects their spouses and most of all their children. Sadly, those in charge of overseeing how these cases are handled, like the United States attorney general and his DOJ, don't care about the impacts on these families as long as they meet their "quota" of rounding up as many Trump supporters as possible. I can only imagine that the attorney general does so with the hope that it will lead to the arrest of the former president himself. I bet to him, that's all that matters.

The current administration, and some previous ones too, want revenge on Trump so badly because he upset the applecart so to speak. It is clear that the current DOJ will stop at nothing to take him down. We as Americans are watching this unfold in real time. When you think about this whole debacle, the message being sent and received is that certain political party members would rather cause pain and destruction to the American people because of their political inclinations rather than take action to protect the rights that are engraved in our country's foundation. It's really disturbing to know that we live in the greatest country in the world, the free world, and many Americans' votes, thoughts, words, opinions, and party affiliations are being denied. Due process denied!

THE JAILS

January 6 has been very eye-opening. Before this day, I was living, what I suppose you could say, a normal life. It was more normal than the life I am living now, that's for sure. I have always been interested in current events and the state of affairs in our country. I am very open-minded, and I feel very deeply. Most would say that I am an extremely compassionate person. I hurt when others hurt, even if they are my nemesis. Over the course of these past twenty-one months, I have seen and heard a lot. This experience has been life-altering in many ways. I can say unequivocally after watching the hell this DOJ has put Tim through and hearing from other detainees both related and unrelated to January 6 that we have a serious issue within our jail system in this country.

It's unfortunate to say that we have many politicians who offer a lot of lip service about prison reform and fixing the broken jail system but never produce any results. I can say further that a lot of what we read, hear, and watch on the news doesn't provide all the information needed to form an informative perspective or opinion on a topic. We all know the media hates Trump and broadcasts biased news to compensate for that hate. It's truly disheartening that this whole January 6 fiasco is about revenge on one person.

Now let me be very clear, this chapter may be a bit controversial, but I make no apologies about my opinions. They are mine, and that is the beauty of living in the free world, or at least I think we do. On that note let's just dive in.

The first thing I think you need to know is that the area where the J6 detainees were being held was an allegedly closed section of the jail that was only reopened coincidentally a week before January 6. Of course, this could simply be happenstance, but I find it to be a bit tactical to say the least.

Tim was arrested on January 15, 2021. He was taken into custody and brought to our local county jail in New Jersey. From there he was transferred to another county jail in a different part of the state. He was then picked up and brought to New York, then to Oklahoma. From there he went to West Virginia and on to Virginia, before finally landing in DC CTF, where the conditions have been brutal.

Upon Tim's arrival, he contracted COVID. He couldn't make bond, and yet in our home state the governor was releasing actual criminals, some of them rather dangerous, in response to the coronavirus. The hypocrisy is maddening. This was the case for most of the J6 detainees. How sad that these defendants couldn't be in their home states if they had to be jailed until trial. But we all know this was just another way to afflict more hardship on these defendants and their families; another way to punish them for their support of a president they admired. It always seemed that the DOJ was trying to "shock and awe" us with their next moves.

In case you didn't know, there is a difference between jail and prison. Jails are located in a county, state, or even a city and are considered a temporary holding facility for a new arrestee. Jails are where the defendants who are not eligible for bond are held while awaiting trial or sentencing. Sometimes a defendant can be held in jail if their sentence is one year or less, but usually once a defendant is sentenced, they are moved from jail to prison.

Prison is governed by either the state where the crime was committed or the federal government if a federal crime is committed. If the defendant is found guilty of a federal crime and has to do prison time, a federal judge can make a recommendation of where that defendant should do his or her time. Ultimately the Federal Bureau of Prisons can decide where the defendant will serve the time. Right now, we are awaiting Tim's transfer to prison, and we asked the judge for consideration of bringing him closer to home. Luckily, the judge agreed, but now we wait to see if the BOP will oblige. You can only pray that these January 6 defendants will serve their prison sentences in their home states or very close to it. Unfortunately, not all will have this desired outcome.

Tim and the other DC detainees have endured severe solitary confinement; they call it a 23 and 1. Twenty-three hours per day in a cell and one hour out to shower and make a call, for six months straight. In June 2021, that twenty-three hours went to maybe twenty hours per day in a 5x5 cell. And while they had a few more hours of recreational time, the fact remains that many men and some women with no criminal history and no violent charges were kept in solitary confinement for more than one year. That is the case for anyone sitting in the DC CTF jail.

As I said, this past year and a half has been extremely eye-opening. Given what I am learning about the current state of our systems, I am utterly alarmed, and you should be too.

In this very country, we are jailing young kids who come from really rough circumstances and backgrounds. While there may be some efforts in place within the jail and prison systems, it is not enough. During the time that Tim has been in the DC jail, I have not been able to speak to a social worker, medical personnel, or an ombudsman. I can't get answers to questions; it's impossible for him to receive mail. There is no clergy available to him, no online classes, and no counseling. There are no in-person visits allowed and no video visits. I can count on one hand how many times he has seen the sun since he has been taken hostage. His health has declined, and he has not seen a dentist in over a year. I wish I could say that January 6 is the reason for this, but unfortunately, this is the reality of how our jail systems function.

Some jail or prison personnel treat detainees like they are beneath them because they have broken the law. Now don't get me wrong, that statement is not a broad one, and evil does walk among us. Sadly, some prisoners must be kept at bay, but I am talking about those who have broken the law for the first time or who are being held as a political prisoner, or a young person with a sad home life who does foolish stuff that lands him or her in jail often. Why are we not working overtime to rehabilitate these individuals? Every resource that we can provide should be available! There should be so much education available to low-tiered offenders, especially first-time ones. Facilitating family interaction should be a top priority! Mentorship and religion are two nonnegotiables that should not be optional. All of this and more should be mandatory, even in the face of a pandemic!

I get many calls from J6 detainees, and when I ask what they are doing to pass the time, the answer is always nothing, simply because nothing is available. When they are not in solitary confinement, what is there for them to do since nothing is available? Why are our Republican politicians so quiet on this? Or why are our Democratic politicians not fighting for no-cash bail for this group of detainees as they do for others? When the politicians in this country are more concerned with playing politics than looking after the youth and those most in need, we must act! There are so many children impacted by the events of January 6 and our politicians are not speaking on that. Children of the detained and also defendants who were still in their teens when arrested are struggling from the fallout of January 6. This was a life-changing event and may have catastrophic implications that could very well change the life trajectory of a young person. We must do all that we can to help provide as much support as possible and ensure there are things in place to help long term. We must be the people of action. I think the average American, such as myself, can and would do more than a person elected to Congress or even the presidency for that matter. I am a person of action, and I am writing about my actions in this book and hope that many more will stand with me and begin to act. The state of our country at current is pretty grim, and after watching this mess, I am more determined than ever to do my part and bring the action!

 Many men and women have suffered from serious medical issues throughout their time in jail and haven't been allowed to see a doctor. Their complaints fall on deaf ears, or they are just blatantly ignored. Some of the prison guards are so full of hate that they just treat these men and some women with contempt.

The conditions in the cells are horrendous, with black mold, discolored water with a metallic taste, and sewer backups. In DC these men have been woken up and forced out of their cells to clean up "shitty" water. They've been called to clean up this foul water when it's been up to their ankles. This exposure to such rancid and bacteria-infested water can only prove to have adverse health effects. These conditions are unacceptable, and again this is not only a January 6 issue.

Not only are the jails disgusting, but they're also inoperable. There have been multiple times when the phones were not working effectively, and calls could not be made. Imagine a husband not being able to call his wife, a father who can't speak to his son, and more importantly, a defendant who can't talk to their lawyer. How is this allowed?

Plus, the library has been unavailable, so they can't even occupy their time educating themselves. What is the point of sending people to jail or prison if they can't even take the actions necessary to make self-improvements?

And how about that controversial deputy warden at the DC jail? She hates the January 6 detainees, and she makes no bones about this. She has mistreated them in every way imaginable. She is clearly unable to be objective with these men and women and incapable of treating them with regard. We know from seeing her social media accounts that she is a major Trump hater, and even worse is that she hates Trump supporters that much more. How can someone like this be running a jail of diverse men and women, as well as those with different cultural and political views? The answer is she in fact is not capable! To quote Representative Marjorie Taylor Greene, "This deputy warden is perpetuating a two-tiered incarceration system where Caucasian pre-trial detainees are mistreated especially if they are a supporter of the previous president." This deputy warden even went so far as to lock out members of our very Congress from entering the jail. In a conversation I had with some of these members of Congress, they discussed how horrified they were when they saw the conditions of those being held at DC CTF, and not just January 6 inmates but more or less the entire facility. How shameful and even more concerning. In my perspective and (unprofessional opinion), this deputy warden has stoked the already high tensions we are dealing with in this country as it is. She is adding to the issues we face as a nation and does nothing to help with the change. We can't create change if we're choosing a side over the people. Being a responsible party for furthering division, stoking fear, and spewing and regurgitating hate does nothing for the very things a person like this deputy warden complains of. Stop the finger-pointing!

On Veterans Day 2021, there was an incident in the DC jail. Now keep in mind that the majority of January 6 defendants in the DC jail were active or reservist military or veterans. So, on this Veterans Day, there was a dispute over a mask between a female guard and a January 6 detainee. This female guard became so enraged with the detainee because he wouldn't wear a mask that she unloaded several cans of Mace or bear spray (whatever you choose to call it) and filled the entire pod with fumes. She had a gas mask on, but the men were dropping to their knees and several of them were taken out on stretchers.

I remember when Tim called home that day and told me what he had experienced and witnessed. He was horrified at how veterans were treated that day, as we should all be showing our gratitude and regard to them for their service. Many were locked in their cells at the time of the incident. They had extreme difficulty in breathing, their eyes became terribly irritated, and one detainee became so overwhelmed by the fumes he passed out and was taken out on a stretcher after falling and hitting his head: all of this over a mask!

This should make everyone in this country uncomfortable. We are watching a two-tiered justice system be created, and if you are not on the right side of the majority and you oppose a certain political party, this is what you will face. It is very alarming when you take the time to read the information that is out there and learn just how broken our nation is becoming.

Another issue in some of the jails, if not most of them, is the lack of nutrition. I will go back to the DC jail specifically, as this jail pertains mostly to January 6 detainees. These men and women have been eating bologna sandwiches every single day. They'll also get a rotation of hard-boiled eggs and cheese sandwiches. Some days when food choices are limited (as if they were not already limited enough), these men will get several pieces of bread with condiments and nothing to spread the condiments on but the bread. If they're lucky, frozen mixed vegetables are served, so at least they get a few nutrients there. On other days they might get an apple or a cup of canned fruit. Ultimately, they have very few nutrient-dense foods, are lacking natural vitamins in their system, and are served unbalanced meals.

By feeding detainees such meals, are we saying that those who are accused of a crime or found guilty of a crime deserve to be treated differently? A young eighteen-year-old with a rough upbringing who made some wrong decisions that landed them in a youth detention facility or the county jail shouldn't be looked down upon or treated differently. The initial reaction of many is to overlook or look down on an individual like this because it seems like a waste of time and resources to invest in helping them and their future. That is wrong! Jail and prison shouldn't be a place where you sit and rot for that one mistake you made in your life. It should be a place where you reflect on the damage that you have done and serve your time for your actions, get educated to find and practice ways to change your mentality and behaviors, and have the support and encouragement from others to change your life and become a stronger, smarter, and more driven American.

We should be teaching our youth that they are important, that their brain is important, that what they think is important, that what they need is important, and that their bodies are important and deserve to be invested in. I have received many letters since starting this foundation from non-January 6 defendants; the letters are sad. They let me know that they feel a sense of hope when they learn that something or someone is out here trying to create change. I am motivated every single day to work for change and be a person of action. Our future and the futures of our children and grandchildren deserve a better tomorrow. Unfortunately, they never will with the state of affairs we all face in this country right now.

What's left for us all to do is to pray. When the men endured solitary confinement, there was nothing for them to do but pray. Imagine twenty months in jail, languishing in solitary confinement, denied fundamental human rights, one of them being your right to practice religion. Living in the harshest of conditions and anxiously waiting to learn your fate is so painful, but to face it without your clergy makes it even more terrifying. I know when I got the first call from Tim after he had been arrested, the first thing he asked me was "Can you please get me MY Bible?" Tim didn't want any other Bible; he wanted his own. His connection to God has always been strong, and his first request as a man held in pretrial detention proves that.

I quickly called that jail in New Jersey to make sure he got a Bible. This most wonderful woman made sure he got a Bible, although it could not be his own. At the beginning of this, the Bible is what he knew would get him through. As time passed and he realized he was not going to get the religious support he so desperately wanted and needed, he brought the word of the Good Book to himself. Tim and the many others just existing in the jail knew they didn't need clergy to connect to God, so they created their own Bible study and sought the Good Book in all they did. They found many scriptures that helped ease some of their pain and heartache, and they drew comfort knowing their families were connecting to the Good Book too on the outside.

Prison ministry is so important and vital and how dare any jail system deny these defendants the right to meet with their clergy? To this very moment as I write this, there is still no prison ministry available to these men and women in jail. The Good Book tells us this about ministering to those incarcerated in Matthew chapter 25 verse 36–40—"I needed clothes and you clothed me, I was sick and you looked after me, I was in prison and you came to visit me. Then the righteous will answer him, 'Lord, when did we see you hungry and feed you, or thirsty and give you something to drink? When did we see you a stranger and invite you in, or needing clothes and clothe you? When did we see you sick or in prison and go to visit you?' The King will reply, 'Truly I tell you, whatever you did for one of the least of these brothers and sisters of mine, you did for me.'"

The Good Book is all some of these defendants have to get them through. Some do not have anyone on the outside, so visiting with clergy is crucial and should be an essential part of anyone's incarceration.

For those of you reading this little book, I ask that you please lift up all those incarcerated in prayer. If you follow the Good Book, then you know no matter what the crime is there is truly only one judge. Christ Jesus and his word say this in 1 Corinthians 4: 3–4 (King James Version): "But with me, it is a very small thing that I should be judged of you, or of man's judgment: yea, I judge not mine own self. For I know nothing by myself; yet am I not hereby justified: but he that judgeth me is the Lord."

Psalm 69: 33: "The Lord hears the needy and does not despise his captive people."

Hebrews 13: 1–3: "Keep on loving one another as brothers and sisters. Do not forget to show hospitality to strangers, for by so doing some people have shown hospitality to angels without knowing it. Continue to remember those in prison as if you were together with them in prison, and those who are mistreated as if you yourselves were suffering."

THE FAMILIES

A family doesn't need to be perfect, but it must be united. Many families were in peril after hundreds of arrests in early 2021. Women were left in dire straits after the loss of income from their spouses' long-term detainment. Some of these women had nowhere to turn. After Tim was arrested, the weeks seemed to drag on, and I couldn't get any information about his situation. It was very frustrating. I had to rely on Tim's lawyer for information.

When J6 families need to rely on anti-Trump public defenders, the information they get is sparse and selective. The jails were denying legal calls as well as in-person visits between the defendants and their attorneys. As I am writing this entry in late 2022, the DC jail is still denying visits to family members. Families are constantly in a state of uncertainty and anxiety. I realized that there needed to be a place to turn and find comfort, a place to connect with someone who knew exactly what they were feeling. That place for connection needed to be a judgment-free zone. To me, it was obvious that a community was needed to support families through this nightmare of an experience.

At the beginning of this "fedsurrection" the J6 families were left with the task of investigating all updates and information themselves in order to keep the defendants informed. I am a very family-oriented person, and maybe that's why I could no longer stand by and watch the horror show of confusion, anxiety, and isolation for the J6 families. We needed to start a community for J6 families to support each other through this time of limbo and impending doom that was being felt.

One night as I reflected on the hand of cards life had dealt Tim, I was feeling so frustrated and worried. The sadness I felt for him was painful, and I couldn't even begin to imagine what he was feeling. I thought about the many others feeling grief like myself, and I just knew I had to act. I thought about the times in my life when I needed to connect with others in similar circumstances and thought there needed to be a place of support to turn to, and so I decided to start a family-support group.

I told Tim about my vision for the support group, and he was eager to help. He gathered contact information from those he was incarcerated with for me to contact on the outside. Once I had the list from Tim, I got to work. I called each family member, introduced myself, and shared my thoughts about the proposed group. I got a great response! I started a private group chat and created weekly support calls to connect virtually. Word got around quickly, and the support group grew quickly.

Each week we would meet virtually and support each other. We would share information on family needs, fundraising tips, and what the media was currently covering on J6. These weekly calls became a necessity. In fact, after all this time later, the calls still provide a lifeline of support for many.

It was comforting to connect each week with others who were in the same boat. I looked forward to every call. Over time, I got to know each family more intimately. I would learn about them, their loved ones languishing behind bars, and the many children so burdened by this mess. I also learned about the raids upon the homes of these families, often occurring at gunpoint. It was very disheartening, but at the same time it's been inspiring getting to know many of them. I'd like to introduce you to a few of them right now.

Jack Wade Whitton Family

Wade has been languishing in an ICE facility for more than one year. He was forced into an egregious plea deal, and he now faces many future years in prison. Wade's family unit is small, and so is his partner's. She is such an amazing human being. She is so strong and an absolute fighter, but she is in great pain. At around 6:00 one morning their home was raided, and this marked the first day of Wade's arrest. Was it really necessary to send tens of law enforcement vehicles and agents to this man's house? Was an armored tactical vehicle (ready to destroy anything in its path) truly needed? When I watched the videos of this early-morning raid and I saw this woman in pajamas being led out of her home at gunpoint with her hands high in the air, it turned my stomach.

Imagine being woken up from a deep sleep in the heart of winter and led out of your home in your pajamas. In the cold air, you're forced to your knees on the freezing ground with shotguns aimed directly at your face. How will she ever forget that moment? This has changed her forever. She was immensely traumatized and now suffers from post-traumatic stress disorder (PTSD) and has nightmares.

This couple has lost so much. Wade worked hard to build a fencing business, and now it's gone, just like that. Wade has no criminal history worth noting. He will have to rebuild his business from the ground up upon his release. His life plans are on hold, all because of political theater. I took this young woman under my wing and provided as much comfort as I possibly could. We visited during Christmas 2021, as I wanted her to know that she would never be alone in this.

One of the saddest things I learned from her was that since her separation from Wade, she struggles to sleep soundly night after night. The memory of that horrific moment when her world was turned upside down is engraved in her mind and is too much to bear. It took her a very long time to sleep in her bed with the fear that now lives within her (and without her partner by her side). The scars of that day remain deep within this woman, but I know that with her incredible tenacity and strength she will survive it. And here's a message just for her. "You've got this, Hurricane!" (Wink wink.)

Chris Worrell Family

I connected with Chris's girlfriend pretty early on. She is another very strong woman caught up in this mess. It took a while for her to feel comfortable with me, but now our connection is incredibly strong compared to this time last year. She has become a good friend. She had a lot to deal with during Chris's detainment. She lost her job for speaking out about Chris and the conditions of his incarceration; she exposed his mistreatment and the lack of medical attention he received.

Chris has been battling cancer for many years and was in remission when he went to jail. During his time in "DC Gitmo" he started experiencing some medical issues he had been battling off and on for years. When Chris had a fainting spell in his cell and suffered a fractured wrist, he received no medical care. Fortunately, Chris finally made bond after the judge in his case was made aware of what was happening to him.

Since his release, I have become very close with his girl. I stay very connected with her and check on Chris often. I am sad to report that Chris's cancer has returned, and chemo treatments have resumed. In addition, Chris has been battling a new medical condition and has been hospitalized on multiple occasions. He recently had a surgery that involved a painful recovery. So much has been taken from this family, with the decline in Chris's health being the biggest of all. He has serious conditions of his release and cannot leave his home. We pray that by the time this book is released, we will be reporting great news on Chris's health as well as the outcome of his case.

Ken Harrelson Family

I connected with Ken's wife several months into this nightmare. She had a lot on her plate with Ken facing very serious charges on the Oath Keeper indictment. By the time you read this entry the verdict will have been determined in Ken's case and he will hopefully be found not guilty. My hope is that he will be back at home with his wife and children, but if not, then Ken will be awaiting sentencing by the time this book is available to the public. Ken has had a lot of losses, like all the J6 defendants. He has had custody issues, loss of VA benefits before his charges were even adjudicated, and the long separation from his wife and children.

Ken's wife and I have become great friends. She has volunteered so much of her time in helping me get the original PFP website up and running. She was so helpful at the beginning of our project, and she still volunteers her time when needed. She lends a hand to anyone in need. I know in a lot of ways her helping the many families has helped her in return.

We finally got to meet face-to-face in DC at Ken's trial when I went to provide moral support for her and the others going through the same hellish experience. Imagine a wife not seeing her husband for more than one year and then seeing his face for the first time. It's a very emotional moment, and even then, she was told that he was not permitted to speak to or look at her.

During the first week of Ken's trial, she decided to write him a love note. Just like you would pass a note to your school friend, she passed the note to their lawyer who showed it to Ken. The US marshal babysitting Ken seemed to have a mental breakdown over this innocent note. He gave it to the judge, who read it aloud in court! "Hey, my love!" and so on and so on. Why the big deal? Well, the judge agreed it was no big deal, but he warned her not to do it again. OK, I get that federal court has rules, but what do you expect of these women who are missing their partners?

Thomas Caldwell Family

I just love Tom's wife. She is such a sweetheart and a peaceful warrior. She is a true fighter. I know this government is not taking her husband without a fight! Tom is such a big teddy bear. I just love him. He has many medical ailments and a recent surgery, but his fighting spirit is strong. Tom is a retired lieutenant commander in the United States Navy. After serving this great country for twenty-five years, this is the thanks he gets.

Tom never even went inside the Capitol, but because of some "big talk" and a few text messages where a bunch of young kids refer to him as "Commander Tom," he suddenly finds himself being hailed the leader of the Oath Keepers! Due to the way these texts have been framed, he could face many years in prison. Tom's wife is not allowed in the courtroom during trial in this case, until she gives her testimony on Tom's behalf, so Tom must go through most of his trial alone. The support within the courtroom is small for these defendants. I have been attending the trial on and off in support of the defendants and making sure Commander Tom has support in his wife's absence.

What I witnessed during his trial was tragically comical. The entire case of the prosecution is based on hearsay and text messages. I hope people truly understand what's at stake in these cases for the defendants and their families. I pray that when all is said and done, Tom will have been deemed not guilty.

Kyle Young Family

When I connected with Kyle's spouse, I was horrified when I learned what she was doing to earn extra money after Kyle was detained. I learned that she would donate plasma just to get enough money to pay her bills. What has our country come to when a woman must donate plasma to make extra money? Andrea works overtime to support her family due to the lost income since Kyle's arrest and she still struggles tremendously.

I guess whichever way the wind blows that day will determine how the judges will treat you, even with the future of your life hanging in the balance. Why did some people on Kyle's indictment get bond, but he didn't? Why do only some with violent charges get bond and some with none are denied? On the day of Kyle's sentencing, while his wife and mother were present in the courtroom, his accuser proceeded toward Kyle and very angrily told him, "I hope you suffer." Was that necessary? Weren't the eighty-seven months he got enough torment and punishment for this poor man?

I spoke with Kyle's wife shortly after the sentence was handed down, and it was heartbreaking. The punishment of January 6 defendants goes way beyond the defendant. Kyle's wife was forced to plan the next several years without her husband by her side. If that wasn't enough, the Bureau of Prisons placed Kyle in a prison more than ten hours away from their home. For the next several years, Kyle's wife will be traveling those ten long hours to visit him. After many of these instances, it seems like these types of decisions are made to further punish J6 families.

Robert Morss Family

What can I say about my friend "Lego Mom"? She is so brave and has endured many things since her son's arrest. Her heart is big, and she is always willing to lend a helping hand. She is standing by her son and is doing everything she can to fight for his release. She has come to many of PFP's events to speak out for her boy, and she continues to advocate for him whenever she can. She has become family to me.

When Tim was being sentenced, she found it in her heart to accompany me and support us during the sentencing. Imagine being the proud mother of a highly regarded Army Ranger (who served his country on multiple tours of duty) only to see your very own government throw your son into solitary confinement. Robert was moved from DC Gitmo to Warsaw, Virginia, after he was assaulted by several guards. While he gets to have video visits with his mom, she still cannot see him in person because visits are not permitted due to COVID protocols. If a detainee and their loved one are not vaccinated, no visits will be permitted.

Robert is a history buff who has a great love of Legos, hence the nickname "Lego-guy." Robert is an absolute sweetheart whose faith is bigger than this fallen world. He helps everyone in need in that jail, and he is always eager to lend a helping hand. I look forward to the story Robert will share upon his release, which I know will become a great book.

Paul Hodgkins's Story

Paul's case is sad and frustrating. He was charged with the ridiculous and now infamous 1512 charge, "obstruction of an official proceeding." If Paul had not been hit with this charge, he likely would not have seen the inside of prison.

We are talking about a man with no criminal history, no violent charges, and no assault charges, who has now been hit with a felony charge. It's sickening that the DOJ is on a mission to create as much "shock and awe" as possible and will not stop until these men get the jail time the department is so desperate to stick them with. It's the DOJ's strategy to charge as many J6 defendants as possible with this felony so that they will be imprisoned.

This charge of obstruction was weaponized against Paul and many January 6 defendants. These prosecutors threaten lengthy jail time if the defendants are found guilty at trial in hopes they will take a plea deal. The prosecution in Paul's case was determined to obliterate his life, and in fact that's exactly what they did. Paul served eight months in prison after taking a dreadful plea deal, all because he supported a president whom he loved dearly.

Paul protested an election that he believed had some inconsistencies. Paul, like many, got caught up in an emotional moment, yet he didn't hurt anyone or anything. Nevertheless, he lost eight months of his life and so much more.

Not only did he need to serve time, but Paul was also labeled a domestic terrorist. Since his arrest, he's lost his job, home, and beloved cats. I connected with Paul through Geri Perna after his release. She was so upset for Paul and told me what he was enduring since his incarceration. I contacted Paul immediately, and I am happy to report as I write this entry that he is taking his life back and doing great! He will not let this travesty define him or his future. PFP is here to support Paul and the many others facing the same fate.

Pollack Family

Ben and Tina Pollack are mom and dad to Olivia and Jonathan, who went to the Capitol on January 6 and were arrested. Olivia is out on bond with an ankle monitor, and Jonathan is on the run.

The Pollack family is very religious and active in their community, and Ben does prison ministry. The family home has been raided several times now, and the FBI is offering tens of thousands of dollars for information leading to the capture of Jonathan. In the first raid, one hundred plus agents showed up to the Pollack's ten-acre farm. There were seventy-five to one hundred police cars. The streets were blocked off for miles. There were three armored trucks that appeared to be military-style tanks. Flash-bang grenades were thrown at all houses on the property, which broke out windows and left burn marks on the carpet and tile floor. One was thrown in the bathroom and burned the porcelain tile off the wall.

Other family members of Ben and Tina also live on the property in their own houses. They said that due to the number of grenades thrown, they assumed that Ben and his family were dead. Family members had to crawl on the ground due to the effects of these grenades. They thought they were going to die! Can you imagine the terror for this family? Several young children were present, including babies, when this home was so violently raided. There was a six-hour search of their property. The search was so thorough that they even pulled off light fixtures from the ceilings, and yet they didn't find anything incriminating.

Despite this type of terror, Ben Pollack's spirit is not broken. He and Tina come on our support calls every week ready to pray. We cannot get off the phone without Ben praying. He prays at the beginning and at the end of all our calls. He is always encouraging us, praying over us, and is incredibly upbeat. He refuses to allow himself to fall victim to the terrorizing trauma of the day of the raid. Ben is one of the biggest reasons why some J6 families come to the support group. He has no problem shedding a tear and will do so without hesitation for what everybody is going through on those calls.

This is a man whose family has been massacred by the media, but he takes all that pain and channels it to help others. Ben has prayed for my nephew Tim. He looks forward to the day that he can lay his hands on Tim and pray with him in person. He's a very selfless and kind soul who is very down to earth and authentic. When I connected with him, I felt a heaviness lifted from me. He always seems to make me laugh. Even so, his heart is broken over what has happened to his family. Despite all these challenges and harassment from the government, nothing has shaken his sense of patriotism. He is a true American.

George Tanios Family

I've met George's mother, sister, life partner, and his three babies. George was arrested and spent a little less than a year in DC GITMO. He was accused of a horrific crime that could have put him in prison for the rest of his life. George was accused of causing the death of Capitol Police Officer Brian Sicknick.

A media frenzy followed the death of Officer Sicknick. Multiple media outlets reported that Officer Sicknick was hit in the head with a fire hydrant. However, George was accused of spraying this officer with some sort of chemical spray. Even though there was no evidence to support this claim, the case had the capacity to destroy George and his family.

George's partner Amanda is another incredibly strong woman who had to navigate life with three babies while waiting to learn the fate of her life partner. Everything she knew was on hold, and her life felt dismantled as she waited to know what could happen next to George.

This family has lost so much, including a successful sandwich shop. But the biggest thing George lost: precious time with his twin babies. In the summer of 2021 when the babies were about to turn one, I received a call from George's partner. She wanted to let me know she was coming to New Jersey and asked if we could meet in person while she visited. I was honored to meet her family! She along with George's mom and sister accompanied Amanda for our visit.

George's mom really broke me down. She cried from the minute she walked in my door until she left. My husband was home that day, and he made me proud. He sat with George's mom and comforted her lovingly. George was her baby, and she felt broken by not knowing how to help her child. We felt ourselves grieving with her.

During my visit with Amanda and George's other family members, we celebrated the twins' birthday. I wanted to provide as much love and support as I could to this woman and her babies. We had birthday cake, wore party hats, and enjoyed some great food from our local Italian market!

Upon her arrival, I was able to share with her that Patriot Freedom Project would be able to help her financially. She was so relieved. George's bond hearing was coming up the following week, so it was a load off her shoulders (even if it was just for a minute). With some help, she felt she could focus on the outcome of George's bond hearing.

During this visit, I was coloring with one of George's children. While we were coloring, this little one described to me how he recalled the raid on his home. (Yes, another violent raid in front of a young child!) This little guy told me that his dad was a bad guy because he had to wear handcuffs. He went on to tell me about his mommy crying during the raid. I was heartsick listening to this story.

We have to make sure this little person does not fear the police or his own daddy. This sweet child had a sharp recollection of what happened to their home, and his mom had a big load to carry with all of this as well.

I am happy to report that by the time this book goes to print, George will be on the other side of this nightmare. George will be sentenced in January 2023.

Rachel Powell Family

I recently visited Rachel Powell, who is on house arrest. There is a lot of controversy and negativity about her and her decision to go to the Capitol on January 6, which would bring so much negative media attention and speculation about her actions on that day. Unfortunately, Rachel made a bad decision on January 6, and that decision cost her dearly. Rachel has been charged with not only the famous obstruction charge but also with depredation of government property. She has no criminal history. She assaulted no one that day. The only person Rachel hurt that day was herself by breaking a window at the Capitol. Should Rachel rot in jail for years over a mistake? Rachel is a mother of eight and a grandmother of three, soon to be four. She is forty-two years young and has lived a challenging life. What I love about women like Rachel is that despite how hard their lives have been, they don't play victim.

I met Rachel and all her children, as well as her grandchildren, and I was profoundly moved by her beautiful family. She homeschooled her children and is still homeschooling her little ones, ages six, eleven, and fourteen. She lost her home, job, and custody of her children when she was first arrested. Being separated from her babies was very painful and difficult for her. She was forced to undergo a ton of evaluations to prove she was a fit mother. I sat with the kids to learn more about them and how this life-changing event has impacted their lives.

I brought the kids some goodies (from the amazing donors of Patriot Freedom Project). Listening to her children was very distressing for me. They are scared for their mother and for what lies ahead. When Rachel was first released from prison, she was still living in her own home. Anti-J6ers found out where her family lived and began harassing and threatening them. It became a very worrisome situation.

Due to the harassment, she was forced to sell her home and move to keep her children who still live at home safe. Of Rachel's eight children, five still live at home. Thankfully, after the move she and her kids are now in a much safer location. Rachel is on a very strict house arrest, and she can't even go out the front door. She can't check her mail or even walk into her yard to enjoy the fresh air and sunlight.

The chief judge who gave Rachel bond imposed on Rachel several conditions she had to meet, including that she must wear a mask inside her own home whenever her young children were present. That's right—her own children wouldn't have been able to look at their own mother's face because of a mask. COVID is always a convenient excuse for imposing more punishment and hardship on J6ers. In my opinion some of these judges have such contempt for J6ers. They just don't care about any of these people and their lives, families, or future.

When one of Rachel's daughters got married recently, she was not allowed to attend the wedding, and she will not be present when her daughter gives birth any day now.

Her other daughter recently had a baby, and she couldn't be there for that either, which is all devastating. Her grandbaby is facing a very serious surgery, and she cannot be there to support her daughter and grandchild. Her not being able to attend such major events in her children's and grandchildren's lives is wrong. She cannot help or be there for her girls (as any mother desires to) during these important milestones. As mentioned, Rachel has no criminal history and is not a danger to society in any manner, despite what the overzealous prosecution would have you think.

The judge in her case loathes her so much that you can visibly detect it at her hearings. In her most recent hearing, the judge was upset that Rachel's lawyer requested a continuance. Unprofessionally, the judge just got up and walked out of the hearing! Rachel will never see fair treatment or a fair trial. The Patriot Freedom Project has helped Rachel get a new lawyer to replace the public defender who needed to go. PFP will continue to support her until she and her children are fully intact again.

Perna Family

I remember the night I got the call that Matthew Perna had died by suicide. It was late on a Saturday night on what had already been an emotional weekend for me. Unfortunately, my family and Geri Perna's family have suicide in common. The night I received this heartbreaking phone call just happened to be the anniversary of my own loved one's passing by similar means.

I couldn't believe I was getting this tragic phone call on this particular day of all days. I knew I had to connect with the Perna family immediately. I waited a few days before I contacted Geri. When I finally connected with her, I learned that Matt had walked through an open door at the Capitol just like Tim had and was inside the building for just a few minutes. Matt was arrested after he voluntarily turned himself in soon after.

Geri described the next year as a "living hell" for Matt. When I finally contacted Geri after learning the sad news of Matt's passing, I promised her I would help her through the devastation. I've had five years to adjust to the aftermath of suicide, and I wanted to share with Geri what has helped our family recover, or at least what has helped us cope.

Unfortunately, I understood what this family would be facing. It took some time for Geri to become comfortable with me, but we have become like family. Matt's family recently honored him with the First Annual Matthew Perna Freedom 5K run, sponsored by Patriot Freedom Project, and it had an amazing turnout! I had the honor of meeting the entire Perna family, including Matt's father. They are a wonderful and amazing family. Matt's dad is brokenhearted and had already suffered a profound loss when his wife passed away earlier in life.

How much more should this family lose? If the DOJ and the prosecution in Matt's case had their way, it would be everything! They are such a loving and close family. I so enjoyed spending time with them and learning about how truly unique Matthew Perna was. Geri has been a great help and so supportive of the Patriot Freedom Project as well, and I am grateful for her friendship.

Geri and I will be connected forever; our nephews are together in paradise shining their beautiful heavenly lights upon us and our brothers. We are soul sisters! The Perna and Hughes families are forever connected. Love you, Ger.

(See Chapter 11, "Matthew Perna," for Geri's perspective on Matt's tragic experience.)

Why We Support the Families

I have a lot of heartache over Tim's incarceration, but it is a little different from what many of these families are enduring (especially the wives). Tim has been a metaphorical prisoner (in so many ways) almost his entire life. I had been grieving this before January 6. I know how profoundly strong Tim is, and I am sad that he has been forced to endure an additional trial in his life.

My ex-husband spent a lot of time in and out of jail, leaving me to figure things out all the time on my own. Things like rent, utilities, food, birthdays, Christmases, and so much more. I was always resourceful and turned to my community when in need. There was always a "Patriot Freedom Project" type of organization or person around to lend a helping hand. I knew there was a need for community and connection, and I thought back on the people and places I had turned to in times of need. I just wanted to do my part and extend the favors outward. I knew I would be a good fit for this, so I jumped into action to help these incredible families through a very debilitating time. I have formed great connections with so many amazing people. I t's an extremely humbling feeling when you know you have helped so many.

We will be dealing with trials, sentencings, and a lot of hardship in the foreseeable future, and there will be serious needs to be met. We have recently learned that two thousand new arrests are likely on the horizon! A recent prosecutor said, "They are very early on in the January 6 probe, and it is not an unreasonable expectation to clear out 2,000 cases." Two thousand cases?! I can't believe this!

I'm afraid that the judges and prosecutors are so biased that it blinds them to the impact of the families of these defendants. It's like they cannot see beyond the defendant and refuse to see the destruction to the wives and children. The majority of the prosecutors and judges are anti-Trump. They are biased, and they hate the idea of Trump so much that they will stop at nothing to defeat him permanently. It seems that means going after these J6 families.

I know so many are angry about January 6. None of us are thrilled about what took place that day, especially President Trump. However, the DOJ is throwing people in jail, denying them bond, keeping them in solitary confinement, and obliterating lives because of their hatred for one man. American citizens should never be denied their constitutionally given rights.

According to recent precedent, if this was another type of protest that got out of hand, nobody would be in jail. Right now, children are bearing the burden. They are being displaced from the only home they know, and they are without health insurance because their mom and/or dad lost their job over this mess. I have seen many of these children, and they are struggling as their little lives have been impacted so. The line is crossed for me when children are caused to suffer.

If someone went to the Capitol that day with the intent to cause destruction and harm, they should be held accountable. I do not support violence against any police officer. Last time I checked, we supposedly live in a country where we have due process, the right to a fair and speedy trial in front of a jury of our peers without bias. But that is not the reality on the ground with J6 cases.

People are being held to an entirely different standard over a political witch hunt against President Trump. I try to imagine the other side. If it really was an insurrection and all these people were planning beforehand that they wanted to overthrow the government, I could almost see this type of reaction. Almost. We are still American citizens. We still have constitutionally guaranteed rights, or at least we are supposed to. I could almost see treating people as enemy combatants if they really were trying to overthrow the government. But I don't think that's what the majority were trying to do that day. Many have been jailed and kept in jail when they should have been released, and the judges know it.

Patriot Freedom Project isn't just here to cut a check for new lawyers; it's here to provide community and connection. And that's what we will continue to provide to the many families in need with the graciousness of the true American patriots in this country. It's why we have weekly support group meetings. It's why we will accommodate these families when they must travel to DC to support their loved ones. This is something that many J6 families wouldn't be able to afford without the help of generous Patriot Freedom Project donors. Our whole goal from the conception of PFP was supporting the families, especially the children.

Of course it's important to support the defendants. However, I know helping the families gives these men and women who are deteriorating behind bars some peace of mind. I've received letters from different detainees in the Virginia and DC jails expressing that when their families are being provided for, it does in fact give them immense peace of mind. It takes away a lot of anxiety for people who are already under a lot of stress. When you help the families, you help the defendants. Therefore, it makes sense for us to continue providing support.

I pray I will be able to continue to work hard to help meet the needs of the families as we navigate through this storm. There is still so much wreckage in the lives of many January 6 defendants, and we must continue to grow connections and bring community. After reading this chapter, I hope you will find it in your heart to support our efforts. There very well may be no political solution to this problem until 2024. In fact, I fear many more Trump supporters are about to become January 6 defendants.

PATRIOT FREEDOM PROJECT

In its most concise definition, Patriot Freedom Project is a 501(c)(3) nonprofit organization that was created to support the January 6 community. However, what Patriot Freedom Project encompasses is much more than that. This project came together and rose to the occasion when those who had the ability and power to help didn't. People were in need of support; hence a support group was created with nothing more than the intention to connect and create a sense of community for the many women and children who were facing the fallout of the events of January 6. These wives, and even more so these children, were traumatized as their own government exacted revenge on a political opponent with no regard for the cost to its people.

 From January 2021 through the spring of that year, those being detained in DC Gitmo were held in solitary confinement. For the detainees and their concerned families, it was beyond frustrating to experience. The only source for the families to look to for answers was the news. Sometimes the media would throw us a bone and give us some clarity on what was happening to our loved ones, but most of the time there was nothing. As the days went on, the worry and concern became excruciating, eating at you from the inside out. I was beginning to reach a breaking point.

During Mother's Day and Father's Day of 2021, Tim didn't call me during either weekend. Several days would pass before I would hear something from him. When he would finally call, I would be like WTH, Tim? He told me that he wanted the men to be able to talk to their wives and children during special holidays. He would go on to say that he didn't like to take up the time these men needed by being on the phone when he himself didn't have children. Furthermore, he would express to me his frustration for some of these men and what he was seeing and listening to about the separation between them and their families. This is when I finally realized that there must be something one of us can do to help if our own government won't step up to the plate. That's when I suggested to Tim that we should start a family-support group.

Tim and I put our heads together to make the idea of a support group come to life. He gathered the contact information of the family members of those he was detained with. Once he sent me the information, I started calling the families and asked them to meet me over Zoom. These Zoom sessions quickly grew and became a regular meet-up more than once per week. To this day, the Zoom call is a consistent weekly call and has welcomed many new families.

Over time, other resources were added to enhance the feeling of community for the families, such as private chat groups on some social media platforms. It was amazing to see the friendships being formed and the connections taking place. These women really needed each other, as they were experiencing life as they've never had to before, and who better to understand what they're feeling than other women in the same unbelievable situation? As time went on and we entered summer 2021, I was looking for as many resources as possible to help us all through these very troubling and frustrating times. By the grace of God, my efforts had called the attention of the great Dinesh D'Souza by July 2021.

I remember the day like it was yesterday! I was in the car driving my daughter to a doctor's appointment when my phone rang. The call was from an unknown number. Now, we all know that when we get an unknown number you expect the worst. From telemarketers to scam calls, you always have to err on the side of caution. Thank goodness I took the call that day. When I answered and was told that it was Dinesh D'Souza, I'm not sure how I managed to even pull my car onto the side of the road! He said he wanted to send me a gift to aid in the relief of the January 6 wives and children. Thanks to his gracious donation, soon the Patriot Freedom Project would be born.

By the fall of 2021, Patriot Freedom Project had grabbed the attention of the great Steve Bannon. I then started making regular appearances on War Room, allowing us to reach a much larger audience. Thanks to those appearances, the project has raised over a million dollars! We've also gained endless support. We've received so many letters from patriots around the country who praise the work we are doing, and reading those notes motivates us to keep increasing our outreach even more. Patriot Freedom Project has been able to help so many families because of the generosity and patriotism of so many Americans. We've even had supporters in other countries! As word kept spreading about the organization, many were not afraid to help me and get behind our movement, despite the controversy about Tim and the stigma that was attached to me. For those people, the families and I are so grateful, as having their aid allowed us to continue to raise more money and ultimately help more families.

In the beginning stages of the Patriot Freedom Project's inception, helping families grew from support groups to financial grants. In these early stages, wives were going into the back-to-school and holiday seasons fearing that they'd be unable to afford to make these times special for their children. These mothers were facing the decision of whether to pay their bills to keep their heat on and a roof over their heads or to buy new backpacks for their children to carry their school supplies, buy food to celebrate the origins of our country on Thanksgiving, or buy gifts for their children to open on Christmas. This led Patriot Freedom Project to create the Adopt a 1/6 Family program. We created a page on our site where visitors could select a family to contribute to for the season to ensure that they can enjoy their holiday. The number of gifts and grants these families received because of this program was outstanding. These times were more bearable because of America's combined efforts, and I was filled with so much gratitude that I was able to bring relief to so many.

Eventually, we started getting calls from detainees that they were desperate for a new lawyer to replace the DC public defenders they had been assigned. Unfortunately, the public "pretenders" as we like to call them did not care about the rights of the detainees being denied and were not passionate to help them reunite with their families and regain justice. How could these men and women trust their own lawyers when all they would hear was disparaging comments about President Trump? These detainees and defendants were in this mess because of their love of him, and they needed to be defended by someone who would not make them denounce their loyalty to a president they loved. I knew we needed to figure out a way to help these families connect with committed, hard-working defense attorneys that would give these trials their all. These families were in dire need of financial assistance to pay legal retainer fees.

I soon began to seek advice from professionals and embarked on my journey of navigating the ins and outs of the nonprofit world. After reaching out to and connecting with some of our country's most incredible attorneys, we were able to connect the families to the multiple legal referrals we had accumulated. The January 6 defendants, thanks to these referrals, were able to hire their own attorneys. It was so amazing to see how many people were able to replace their very biased public defenders with attorneys of their own choosing. This opportunity gave the detainees and their families an actual fighting chance against our Department of Justice.

How could any of these defendants possibly have relied on or had faith in the public defenders, when all that these pretenders did was criticize their former president? It was extremely important for these defendants to know that they were in good hands with a lawyer who was willing to fight for them and who would provide them with a fair shot during the trial.

Wait a minute, did I say fair? Oh, don't mind me! There used to be a time that I actually did think there was a shot at a fair trial. Unfortunately, we've come to realize the hard way that a fair trial will never happen in the city of DC in our current state. The inability to receive a fair trial is all the more reason that I went on to create this legal defense fund. These outstanding lawyers have fought very hard to request a change of venue only to be denied every time. All January 6 trials should be litigated outside the city of DC!

We have some of the best lawyers in the country on these cases, and they need our support to continue supporting Americans in need. I have dedicated a part of the Patriot Freedom Project to helping these lawyers continue their efforts. I have developed great relationships with many lawyers and legal professionals and hope to continue connecting with more to help further protect these detainees, as more are being detained each day. I am truly honored to know such great talent in the legal world.

During these twenty-plus months, the previously established legal defense funds have turned their backs on Trump supporters. These same Trump supporters may have something as simple as a misdemeanor charge, which is minor compared to the multiple violations of their amendment rights that they've experienced. That's not even getting into how many Brady violations we have seen so far! For those of you wondering what a Brady violation is, allow me to elaborate for you. It's when this government holds evidence that could be favorable to a defendant's case and that evidence could significantly impact the outcome of one's case. And we already know the prosecutors on these cases do not want to see a favorable outcome in any J6 case. These already established legal defense funds turned their backs on countless people who have asked for and desperately need help. I won't name-drop, but you know who you are, and you're clearly denying American liberties… There are many platforms that have had the opportunity to stand up for these many and multiple amendment violations, but instead they chose to stay complacent. Shameful!

It's astonishing that so many platforms choose complacency when there are clear examples where the treatment of January 6 protesters contrasts dramatically with the treatment of protesters in prior incidents. Laws and justice are clearly bending to the will of those in power, with no regard for the structure and organization that our founding fathers set forth. We've provided research for our viewers that taps into events that have had stark contrasts to January 6. This list of events is ever-growing, and we make it a priority to keep the public up to date with the facts of what is going on, not just what the media wants you to see. We will never be complacent when it comes to justice and doing the right thing, even when it may be controversial. We will also never be afraid to stand up and speak out for our rights as American citizens, our rights that they are trying to take away from us.

Over time, we have connected with many great mental health professionals, who have not only assisted us with our family calls but are also helping us build a mental health community. The need for emotional support is huge given these recent traumatic experiences endured by detainees and their loved ones. I have created an online mental health call for J6 families to connect with these professionals who have been able to provide a supportive, loving ear. We are so fortunate to have these calls on a weekly basis, as so many are benefited.

Through this mental health community, families are learning how to keep moving forward and are creating stronger coping skills. These families are also being taught to navigate through anxiety, PTSD, depression, and most importantly a lot of sadness. These families' lives have been turned upside down by violent raids at gunpoint, leaving children traumatized. The list of endurances experienced by these families is long. This community that the Patriot Freedom Project offers is extremely important and beyond needed to keep these families on the up and up. I know in the hardest parts of my life, I survived by utilizing newly learned coping skills and by creating tools and habits that made me strong enough to pull myself out of that hole—a hole that seems to keep getting deeper when you don't have those mental skills or support. I read somewhere that other people's heartaches can aid others facing hardship. In the hardest times of my life, I had some incredible people lend a helping hand and teach me how to be strong, and now I have the opportunity to pay it forward and bestow the same to these incredible families in need.

Because this hole can continue to get deeper as experiences cause pain and turmoil, it is crucial to create easier access to care, as mental and emotional support should never be a struggle to find. A goal for Patriot Freedom Project is to create a long-lasting mental health community that is not only easy to access but also free. Good health should not be difficult to obtain. Too often when someone is in crisis or struggling, they need a connection like this, and sometimes they don't get it until it's too late. Sometimes in the traditional mental health world, there is just too much red tape.

To boost the morale and mental health of those detained in prisons around the country, we've created a resource where you can go to acquire the mailing addresses of those detained. They welcome and love receiving letters, as it helps keep them in touch with the outside world and also to socialize. In addition to the mailing addresses of those detained, we include pictures of the detainees, some with their families, so that you can see that these are everyday people like you and me who got caught up in this political mess. There is also a link for most detainees where you can learn more about them and what happened to them. The letters written and received have been influential in the continued efforts of both those within the jails to keep moving and those on the outside to keep giving back with gratitude. The benefit that receiving a letter has on an individual when they don't have access to the outside world is huge for their mental health.

One way I've learned to improve my mental health and also my faith is through prayer. Prayer and God have gotten me through the toughest of times, and He will get all those impacted by January 6 through these times as well. The denial of clergy and religion to these detainees is downright disgraceful. As for the families, this is why we've also created a prayer group. Patriot Freedom Project hosts a weekly Bible study and prayer group. The only true way to navigate this trainwreck is through prayer and faith. In these times we must put our trust in God and let him show us the way. Jesus didn't get out of this life without carrying his cross, and we will not either.

MATTHEW PERNA

Note: this chapter was written by Geri Perna, the aunt of the late Matthew Perna. May their story be heard, and action taken to prevent anything like their story from happening again!

Matthew Lawrence Perna came into this world on June 27, 1984. When Matt was two, he developed this strange fascination with the American flag. He would look for flags when riding in his car seat, yelling out every time he spotted one. If a book or a magazine had a picture with a flag in it, he would find it and excitedly bring it to our attention. This fascination obviously did not end when he was young; it continued into adulthood when his patriotism would end up being his downfall.

Matt graduated from Sharpsville High School in Pennsylvania and went on to graduate at the top of his class from Penn State University. He was brilliant in many ways and an avid reader with an extensive library of books. He read constantly and was very well educated on matters of world history and government. He never made anyone feel inferior or stupid for asking questions, and if he did not know the answer (which was rare), he researched and found it. He was a very articulate speaker and writer who loved having conversations with random strangers, especially the elderly. He was always respectful, especially when the conversations revealed differing opinions; he never berated anyone for disagreeing but rather would just smile and agree to disagree (even when he knew he was right).

Matt was adventurous! After graduating college, he worked a nine-to-five job for a few years and eventually signed on to teach English to children in Thailand. He loved it! He formed many friendships during his time there, and when that contract ended, he decided to move to South Korea to continue teaching there. He learned the language wherever he traveled and formed many lasting relationships that he maintained for the rest of his life.

After living in South Korea for a couple years, he learned that his mom, Roni, was given the devastating news that she had leukemia. Matt flew home immediately to help take care of her. He immersed himself completely in learning about holistic remedies, and although Roni was not always a willing participant, Matt did not give up. She was the recipient of a bone marrow transplant, and after almost a year since being diagnosed, she was looking forward to resuming her life. We were all very hopeful and excited that she was out of the woods.

On March 2, 2015, Roni had a regular doctor's appointment during which they did blood tests that indicated she needed blood to regulate her white blood cell count. This was not unusual in the slightest, but what was normally a routine visit turned into a tragic day. The blood she was given had a bacterium present, and Roni was placed on a ventilator; her organs soon began to shut down. She died the following evening with her husband, Larry, and her two sons by her side. It was a tragedy, and the family has never been the same.

Larry was in unimaginable pain from the loss of his wife, and Matt decided to stay close to home rather than returning to his travels. He had no desire to work a nine-to-five job anymore and began marketing alkaline water-filtration machines (something he purchased for his mom when she was ill), essential oils, and eventually Hemp Worx CBD products. He built up a following on social media of over seven thousand people and was networking in his small town and making quite a name for himself. He did not just sell these items, he believed in them. He would never promote anything that he didn't use himself.

When he was selling the Kangen water filtration systems, many people were skeptical. It was an expensive item, but the benefits were well worth the cost. Matt studied the effect of alkaline water on cancer patients and was astounded with the positive outcomes of so many patients. When Matt met people who could not afford the system, but could benefit from the water, he bought dozens of plastic containers and delivered water to them several times a week, at no charge whatsoever. That is the type of person Matt was. He did the same with CBD oil, often just giving it away to people who could benefit from it but could not afford to pay for it. He had a generous heart, and anyone who met him could notice this instantly. However, he did not announce his charitable deeds at all. Only those who witnessed him firsthand knew what a giving soul he possessed. He was humble beyond imagination.

Matt had a strong passion for running and was part of a great group of friends who ran together and participated in many races. He had a wood map made of the United

States, and each state had a hook on it. His goal was to run a race in every state. He had many medals on this map but still had many states left in which to run. He was physically fit and ate healthy foods. Often, he would make some of his "recipes" and share them with his family. He stuck to a very strict diet and exercise routine, and I honestly don't remember him ever having so much as a cold. He did not trust the pharmaceutical industry and wanted no part of supporting it in any way.

Matt traveled the world; it was his passion. He made friends in more places than we will ever know and stayed in contact with them regularly. He sent postcards, no matter if he was traveling or in his home. He took the time to send hundreds, if not thousands, of them and was quite personal with his messages. He wrote beautifully, and each postcard was cherished by the recipient. After Matt's death, many people shared their postcards with me. They had saved them for several years because they had made such an impression on them. He sent them because he liked how he felt when he received one, and he wanted to share that joy with others.

Matt also had a talent for photography and played the piano (a talent that he learned from his dad). His photos were sometimes of random people in his travels or just an object that the average person would have walked by without noticing. Matt noticed everything, and his photography will live on forever. He loved animals, especially dogs. But one day, a kitten that was in poor health wandered onto Matt's porch. Matt, having never owned a cat, began to take care of her. He named her Hinoki, and he brought her back to excellent health using alkaline water and CBD products. She was his roommate; she loved him, and he absolutely adored her.

Before the 2016 election, Matt had been a Bernie Sanders supporter for a few years. However, he changed course and supported Donald Trump in 2016. He attended several rallies, and although he got into some very heated discussions on social media, Matt always kept it civil and respectful. He had this ability to maintain a level of calmness even when he disagreed profusely with someone. When the 2020 election results were announced, Matt was in complete disbelief. He knew the election was stolen and had this tremendous amount of hope that the results were going to be overturned once the truth was revealed.

He decided to attend the Stop the Steal rally on January 6, 2021, with the anticipation of being a part of a historical day in Washington, DC, where the people would have their voices heard and the election would not be certified. He was expecting it to be a day of celebration that would go down in history, and Matt wanted to witness it firsthand. Instead, January 6 was a disaster of epic proportions. Matt was in the crowd of thousands of attendees shoulder to shoulder. As he made his way to the Capitol, he watched in bewilderment as he got closer and saw the crowd waving flags, shouting USA, and making their voices heard, just as his president had instructed. We later learned that Congress had been adjourned at 2:20 p.m. and the building evacuated. Matt entered the Capitol at approximately 2:58 p.m. This point was later presented but had no bearing on the charges he faced. He had no intention whatsoever of entering the building, but the enormous force of the crowds behind him pushed him into a previously opened door and in he went.

There were plenty of instigators in the crowd as well, and these people certainly succeeded in getting the crowd excited. Had it not been for this and the density of the crowd, he would have never gone inside. He was armed with a flag and a cell phone, no weapons of any kind. Once he was inside, the police stepped to the side and allowed the crowds in. While inside, he stayed within the velvet ropes in the Rotunda, recording and chanting "USA, USA!" He touched nothing, stole nothing, broke nothing. He was inside the building for fifteen minutes or less and then exited through the rear of the building.

Matt and his friends returned to their hotel and recorded a seven-minute video talking about their day and what they had witnessed. This same video would later be used against him by the Department of Justice. The video was removed from Facebook, by Facebook, but not before his friend downloaded it. Because of this, we are able to view it now. Matt returned home, and on January 14, 2021, he was informed by a friend that his picture was on the FBI website, and they were looking for him. Matt immediately reached out to a friend who was a retired police officer. He advised him to contact the local FBI office and turn himself in. That morning at 9:00 Matt did exactly that.

The FBI sent two agents to Matt's father's house, where they questioned him about January 6. In hindsight, I wish Matt had retained an attorney before speaking to the FBI. But because the police were allowing people inside the Capitol, Matt did not feel he had done anything wrong. I am fifty-seven years old, and I have been taught my entire life to trust the police, and Matt was taught the same. He told the agents everything, and he thought if he just truthfully explained what happened, it would all be viewed as a huge misunderstanding and that would be the end of it.

Even at that point, he did not feel he had broken any laws. Matt had never had any arrests prior to this incident. In fact, he had never even had a parking ticket in his life.

Matt told the agents exactly what happened that day and everything he had witnessed. He included that he saw several antifa people posing as Trump supporters. They were wearing tactical gear underneath their MAGA attire and were quite easy to identify. After the FBI finished their questioning, they informed Matt that if they thought of anything else, they would be in touch. The agents appeared friendly and kind. Matt treated them respectfully and politely answered every question in detail with his father and uncle present.

I was at my home in Florida during this, and I did not have a good feeling about any of it. I flew up to Pennsylvania that week, and we retained an attorney who came recommended by a friend of a friend. On January 18, 2021, the FBI called Matt and said they had additional questions and were on their way to see him. They obviously phoned from the driveway because seconds later six agents were at his door. Matt voluntarily let them inside the house, where they proceeded to arrest Matt in front of me and his dad.

He was initially charged with two misdemeanors: (1) knowingly entering or remaining in any restrictive building or grounds without lawful authority and (2) disorderly conduct on Capitol grounds. He was taken to the local FBI office in New Castle, Pennsylvania. They searched his home, taking the Trump sweatshirt he had worn that day, along with his cell phones and laptop. This was the beginning of a nightmare for Matt and our entire family, who loved and supported him completely. The local newspaper wasted no time reporting the story with the FBI pictures included. The articles were inaccurate from the start, and although we were called for comments and interviews, we declined every one at the advice of the attorney. The newspaper was notorious for printing false stories, and we knew that our comments would be edited or completely omitted.

The articles upset Matt greatly. Having to explain what happened to his ninety-three-year-old grandfather was very difficult. Facebook and Instagram immediately disabled Matt's accounts, and because of this he wrote a statement and asked me to post it on my pages, which I did. He apologized if his actions offended anyone and admitted to walking into the Capitol with the police ushering him in. After posting this, the backlash began. Friends who had known me since I was five were furious with me and Matt. We were called white supremacists and racists. My classmates publicly shamed me on our group page, of which I was the administrator. We have a reunion every five years, and the page had most of my classmates as members. The comments were awful, and the text messages I received were even worse.

One classmate (with whom I was very close) suggested that it would be best if I removed myself from the group. Matt felt absolutely terrible about this. As I sat crying on the couch as I read these messages, he cried with me. The local newspaper posted the stories about Matt's arrest on their Facebook page as well. The comments were mean, vindictive, and hateful. Many were from friends and relatives, and it was at that moment we realized that very few people were actually our friends. The page is still visible to this day; Facebook has left it visible for all to see. Matt was released later that day, without bail. We met with his attorney, and based on the charges he felt that Matt, who had no prior convictions or any altercations with the law for that matter, would more than likely face a fine and maybe some community service as his punishment. Coupled with the fact that Matt had willingly turned himself in immediately upon hearing that the FBI had posted his picture on their website as a person they were looking for, the attorney assured us not to worry, that he had this.

Unfortunately, that feeling of relief was short-lived. On January 22, 2021, Matt, along with 240 other attendees, were charged with the felony of obstruction of Congress. Matt was then assigned a parole officer to whom he was required to report, and the first of many hearings had gotten scheduled. On February 25, 2021, the grand jury indicted Matt on four counts: (1) obstruction of an official proceeding and aiding and abetting (2) entering and remaining in a restricted building or grounds (3) disorderly and disruptive conduct in a restricted building or grounds and (4) disorderly conduct in a Capitol building. He was arraigned before Judge John D. Bates on March 9, 2021, where Matt pleaded not guilty and was released.

He was more worried than ever; however, his attorney continued to utter his famous words: "Don't worry, I've got this!" However, worry is all Matt and our family could do. Matt's mental condition had begun to rapidly decline, and his father's health was greatly affected by the added stress. Matt had a girlfriend at the time of his arrest. Their relationship became strained because of their differing political views and uncertainty about Matt's future. Shortly after his arrest, she broke ties with him, and this added to his depression greatly. He began talking about suicide, and as each week passed, the news of the mounting arrests of other J6ers concerned all of us even more. It became quite clear that our Department of Justice would stop at nothing to make an example of anyone who was a Trump supporter, especially if they chose to exercise their right to freedom of speech.

He watched as senior citizens were arrested for attending the rally, and when they began incarcerating people who had not even been convicted of a crime, Matt began to feel guilty that he was free to leave his home while others were kept in solitary confinement. Watching the effects that his ordeal had on his dad added to the enormous mountain of guilt he was carrying, and we were all very concerned for Matt's safety. I informed his attorney of our concerns, but I got the feeling he thought I was exaggerating the situation.

Over the next several months several hearings were scheduled. Some were status hearings to present discovery by the DOJ. Almost every single hearing was canceled and delayed. Matt would have himself mentally prepared to attend the hearing only to be informed at the last minute that it was canceled or postponed. The discovery was constantly an issue. As the DOJ continued its search for evidence against Matt, it became quite clear that there simply wasn't anything that he had not already told them. But it didn't matter, as they were out for blood and were not going to stop until they were satisfied.

These delays were devastating to Matt. He simply wanted to put this unfortunate incident in the past and move on with his life. His income had come to a complete halt. He had a huge following on social media where he marketed CBD products as well as alkaline water filtration systems. Without the ability to present podcasts to his audience, his time was spent thinking and worrying about his case. He couldn't seem to focus on anything else. He gave his television away; he couldn't watch the news as it only added to his stress. Matt was suicidal shortly after the felony charge had been added. His emotions were all over the place, and our family was extremely concerned. I again expressed this concern to his attorney but was told that if the prosecution learned of his mental state, he would be immediately arrested and put into a facility indefinitely.

He no longer ran or cared about what foods he was eating. He dove into his Bible, constantly reading and searching for comfort. He saw several counselors and pastors, but none of them could tell him what was going to happen with his case, and it was this uncertainty that consumed him. His hearings never seemed to offer anything new. The prosecution still had not found any additional evidence to substantiate the charges, but the looming threat of additional charges weighed on Matt. He began spending his nights sleeping at his aunt's house because she insisted he not be alone at night. He suffered from terrible nightmares, and his physical health began to deteriorate. As the months passed, we watched in horror as more and more people were arrested for attending the rally in DC. There seemed to be no one who was immune from arrest, except the instigators and obvious antifa members who were present throughout the crowd. Grandmothers, the elderly, veterans, off-duty police officers…all arrested for exercising their freedom of speech. At this writing, over nine hundred people have been arrested so far. This added to Matt's worry. It was more than clear that the DOJ was going to continue its witch hunt and stop at nothing to make examples out of these people who truly didn't believe that they had done anything wrong.

However, there were people at the Capitol who were out of line. Some assaulted police officers and broke things, and they should be dealt with accordingly...but who were these people really? Were they actual Trump supporters? Or were they instigators playing a part? Matt was hopeful at times that the truth would be revealed and charges would be dropped. But every time more people were arrested or stories about the men and women rotting in the DC gulag came out, his hope was diminished. I prayed for Matt constantly throughout my day. Please Lord, make this go away; please reveal the truth and allow these people to be set free! But our prayers were not answered.

The felony charge of obstruction of an official proceeding was the greatest threat in Matt's case. After several plea hearings, it became quite clear that the DOJ had no intention of dropping the felony charge. So, his attorney advised him to plead guilty, in order for this ordeal to end quickly. He told him that there was a chance that the severity of the charges could be lessened if it was proven that Matt needed to take care of his dad. He would possibly have to be on house arrest with an ankle monitor, but at least he would be there for his father. Matt was asked to provide letters about his character and his life to submit to his judge in an effort to ask for leniency. These letters were to be read first by a person in the parole department, who had the authority to drop points from Matt's charges based on the letters.

Matt's dad, Larry, wrote a powerful letter telling how Matt was his caregiver and how one icy evening that winter, Larry had taken his golden retriever outside in the dark for one last evening bathroom time. It was six degrees outside, and there were several inches of snow with a layer of ice on top. He had on a light sweater and had left his phone inside. Larry fell down and was unable to stand. The nearest neighbor lives a hundred yards away, and it was pitch dark. Larry thought he was going to freeze to death. He began crawling on the ice, using his bare knuckles. It took him almost an hour to get to the edge of his yard. At that point, Matt arrived. He had been calling Larry but hadn't get an answer, so he drove there in an ice storm and helped his dad into the house. Also included with this letter was a letter from Larry's doctor confirming his need for assistance.

The woman in the parole department received the letters and the physician's reports and told Matt's attorney that she didn't t believe that Matt was his dad's caregiver or that his dad was in need of one. She declined to take any of the points off, and his attorney told him that because of this, Matt would definitely have to serve time in jail. Initially, Matt was told that he would most likely receive six to twelve months in a federal prison camp in West Virginia. So, on December 17, 2021, Matt entered his plea of guilty. The local newspaper once again plastered his picture on the front page, with inaccurate information as usual. Once again, Matt was the center of attention. Christmas was coming, and with permission, Matt traveled to Florida to spend it with his friend. Christmas night he made his way to our house to spend a few days with us. I couldn't believe how terrible he looked. His eyes no longer sparkled. His smile no longer lit up the room. He was defeated. He was a shell of his former self, and my heart broke for him. He cried many tears while here, and as much as we tried to offer him hope and encouragement, he just wasn't capable of accepting it.

After his plea was entered, he now had to wait over two months for his sentencing hearing. Why? I feel this was just another part of the mental torture the DOJ was inflicting on these people from January 6. Matt began studying federal prison camps. He watched videos and read articles hoping to have his fears lessened. He learned that he could spend his time productively in the camp teaching inmates and helping them obtain their GED. He could continue his education while there and began to feel like he was strong enough to survive this. I told him constantly that the time will pass quickly, and he will come away from this stronger and more successful than he ever thought.

On January 9, 2021, my dad, Matt's grandfather, passed away. I flew home for the funeral, and we decided that the service would be completely private with immediate family only. The reason for this was Matt was so ashamed of himself and didn't want to come to the funeral for his grandfather whom he loved so much if it meant having to face relatives or family friends. Matt attended the funeral and barely said a word. It saddened me so much to see him like this. Matt was this shining light in our family. When he entered the room, everyone smiled. He had such a kind and positive spirit it was contagious. Now, he just seemed deflated, and it was truly heartbreaking.

After the funeral, we took a family photo that included everyone. We have a large family with several nieces, nephews, and grandchildren. This was the last photo we would take while Matt was alive. In hindsight, I wish that I had done more during that visit home. But it was quite evident that

Matt was in a very dark place, and I didn't know the words that would help, as hard as I tried. The month that followed the funeral was particularly rough for Matt. His anxiety as he waited for his March 3 sentencing hearing was increasing by the day. He watched countless videos on federal prison camps and continued spending his nights at his aunt's house. He began to stutter when he spoke; it just came out of nowhere. We later learned that he was vomiting blood and couldn't keep food down. The physical and mental effect this was having on his body was sickening. Why? Because he walked through an opened door at the People's House? His entire life was destroyed because of this.

During Matt's thirteen-month ordeal, we made phone call after phone call to our congressmen and women. We sent dozens of emails to representatives on both sides of the aisle. Not even one phone call was returned or an email answered. Later, our local congressman would deny that any phone calls were logged during that entire time. I know that I personally called at least eight different times. The silence from our representatives hurt Matt so much. He knew that none of them cared about him, and this added greatly to his depression…and mine.

On Monday, February 21, 2022, Matt phoned his attorney to tell him that he had a really bad feeling about his hearing the following week on March 3. You see, March 3 was the seven-year anniversary of his mom's death. I do not believe in coincidences where January 6 is concerned. That date was specifically chosen to add to the mental anguish that Matt was experiencing. Matt's attorney told him that he had bad news. His sentencing hearing was postponed to…April Fool's Day, and the DOJ was going to add a "sentencing enhancement" of terrorism. If the judge agreed, this was going to take Matt's predicted sentence of six to twelve months to forty-one to seventy-two months in a federal prison! Matt did not tell me or anyone else these details that day; we learned of them later.

Matt called me sobbing hysterically on the phone. He kept saying, "I must be guilty," over and over again. He was stuttering so badly I could barely understand him. I kept telling him over and over that God is in control. Don't worry, this is not going to end up as bad as he thought… but again, I did not know about the enhancement at that time. The sentencing enhancement is something that is so unconstitutional, it just blows my mind. Essentially, you are pleading guilty to specific charges, but at the hearing where you have already pled guilty, the prosecution adds additional infractions just before the sentence is announced, all in an effort to influence the judge into giving a harsher sentence. It was this threat that broke Matt completely.

Friday, February 25, 2022, at 6:00 p.m. my phone rang. It was one of my brothers calling to tell me that I needed to book a flight—Matt had just hanged himself in his garage. I went into complete hysterics. I cannot even describe my feelings. My disbelief and anger collided with a sadness so great that my body was in shock. Matt's father, Larry, oh my gosh how would he handle this tragedy? Everything was racing through my mind, and then I called Matt's attorney. I was so angry, and I told him that after months and months of saying, "Don't worry, I've got this"…he didn't have anything! Matt had hanged himself and was dead. His attorney did not believe me! Did he honestly think I would make this up? He finally yelled at me and said that I cannot pin the blame on him for this. He told me that I was irrational and hung up on me. He was heartless and as arrogant as ever.

I flew home to Pennsylvania the following day, writing his obituary on the plane as I sobbed in front of strangers. Our entire family was inconsolable, especially Matt's dad. We planned his funeral, and his obituary went viral. The online guestbook was being signed by people all over the world. The funeral home had never had as many entries before and had trouble keeping up with them. Flowers and plants from strangers all over the country filled the funeral home, and the line of guests seemed never-ending. People we had never met told of us amazing acts of kindness that Matt had shown them. He was so generous and kind, and his many friends were devastated. Matt was so humble, he never spoke of these things to anyone, and knowing that the world lost such a beautiful soul has made our loss even harder to accept.

TRUMP #45

President Donald Trump, the forty-fifth president of the United States and loved by many, has endured more attacks, more disrespect, and more blatant disregard than anything this country has ever seen before. One thing is for sure, no matter how much they throw at this president, he keeps getting back up! Two impeachments; Russia, Russia, and more Russia; the raid on Mar-a-Lago; and of course January 6, a.k.a, the setup by his political opposition.

As the "Unselect Committee" continues their witch hunt against President Trump, he never ceases to bring their twisted narrative back to reality. The reality, of course, is that the election was stolen. The whole reason that over one million Trump supporters attended the Stop the Steal rally on January 6 was that the election was stolen and they had legitimate grievances. "The steal" had a location. It was in the Capitol where the crooked politicians certified the 2020 election without any process of exploring the many legal issues in question or the legitimate concerns of the American People. To ignore the reason for the protest, and to refuse to even acknowledge the election question, shows that for President Trump's enemies, this political conflict has no room for compromise.

From the very beginning of President Trump's candidacy, the political establishment used every weapon at its disposal to try to defeat him, from spying on his campaign to activating media and technology assets against him. However, nothing that the political class tried to pin on President Trump seemed to stick. Try as they might to target him, his family, his businesses, and his inner circle, the most they could do was bog him down in legal disputes. He isn't fazed! The enemy had to attack something very "near and dear" to President Trump: his own supporters.

President Trump's supporters are his greatest treasure and greatest asset. President Trump truly values patriotic Americans, veterans, and loyal supporters more than almost anything else. In many ways, the targeting and detaining of so many of his supporters is a sort of blackmail against him. They, his political opposition, know that is the one thing that would hurt him most profoundly. If the deep state was an actual human entity, you could hear it whisper to President Trump: "Just give up your mandate to lead our country, and we will let them go."

As of this writing, abortion activists, Trump allies, and even President Trump himself have been victims of FBI raids. The whispering continues: "Just give up your mandate to lead this country, and we will stop." But President Trump doesn't negotiate with terrorists. Not with ISIS and not with the deep state. He knows that it's a losing proposition to surrender like that. In truth, they won't ever stop, no matter how many deals they pretend to offer.

Something that has struck me about President Trump's many interviews (even before he was president) was how often he used the word "loyalty." He often explored the idea of the value of loyalty in business and in life. You see, the American people have a pact with President Trump. They believe in him and his policies. They believe that his leadership will result in making America great again. And in return, he uses his skills, knowledge, and power to "drain the swamp" and return power to "the people." The people are loyal to him if he is loyal to them. This pact has not been broken. When he was elected, he followed through with his promises. He brought this country greatness for a fleeting time. When he left the White House, the greatness of our country faded fast enough for all to realize that he and his policies were the determining factors.

The people are loyal to President Trump, not because of his personality, hairstyle, or way of talking, even if those things are very entertaining at times. The people are loyal to President Trump because unlike other politicians who are "all talk," President Trump actually did something to make our nation more prosperous. He actually did something to protect the right to life and to secure the border. He actually did something to stop endless foreign wars. He really took action on the things that "working class" Americans like myself actually care about. So don't count on President Trump to succumb to any blackmail scheme. He has stood strong with the J6 detainees and their families. He has offered solace and support that many people will never know about. It was President Trump who invited the Patriot Freedom Project to his rallies and acknowledged the work that we do. Unlike establishment Republicans who shy away from any difficult topic, President Trump has taken a stand.

On September 1, 2022, Joe Biden gave an "Enemies of the State" speech with ominous red lighting and armed

Marines stationed behind him. He said that MAGA Republicans were extremists and that J6 protesters are insurrectionists despite the fact that no J6er has been charged with insurrection. Biden said, "So tonight, I've come to this place where it all began to speak as plainly as I can to the nation about the threats we face, about the power we have in our own hands to meet these threats." He later said, "We're all called, by duty and conscience, to confront extremists." Don't you love that unity stuff we all heard about? Just a few short weeks later a North Dakota man was charged with murder for the death of a teen whom police say he intentionally hit with a car. A teen that he called a Republican extremist. Unlike many nonviolent J6 defendants, the alleged murder suspect was offered bail and quickly went home; the media, SILENT!

Something I've noticed about President Trump's political strategy is that it involves a lot of patience. He lets his attackers defame him and commit to their lies. Then after the lie is on the record, he comes with a countermove that buries them in their own dishonesty, and it's brilliant! The lies about President Trump and many of the J6 defendants will be exposed, and there will be accountability for those who perpetrated real crimes related to January 6. This accountability will be done "by the book" because, unlike the political class, we "Ultra MAGA" Republicans do believe in the rule of law.

President Trump has not been waiting idly by while the swamp seals the fate of our nation. He has been as busy with his political advocacy and rallies as if he were on the campaign trail. He has dominated the Republican Party so that mostly "America First" candidates remain. The key to power was never just the White House. While his political opposition has attempted to consolidate power through their dishonest narratives, it has only backfired. Just take a look at how the leader of the Unselect Committee (Liz Cheney) did in her home state reelection primary bid. She lost her mandate. All while President Trump consolidated real power behind the scenes by advocating for "America First" Republicans. Thankfully, President Trump is going to work every day to "Make America Great Again," even if his office is temporarily outside the White House.

I thank God that President Trump told his supporters to "peacefully and patriotically make their voices heard" on January 6. I thank God that our movement is a very peaceful one. We can win this political conflict without bloodshed. We have truth, love, and peace on our side. And that means we have God on our side. As Romans 8:31 says, "If God is for us, who can be against us?" As dark as this hour in America is, I know through American principles we can shine a light on it and be the beacon of freedom we were meant to be. God bless America, and God bless President Trump.

—**Sean Morgan** with contributions from **Cynthia Hughes**

HELP—ACTION—RESOURCE

The amazing thing about the Patriot Freedom Project is that is not just bidirectional. We are connected to each other and support each other. It's not just about the money flowing in one direction; it's about community and connection. What better way to heal than with people you've connected with who understand what you have gone through (and are going through)?

The families and defendants have questions about what happens next. What does my future look like? It can be very hard for the defendants and families to find hope amidst the chaos. To help find this hope, we at Patriot Freedom Project give community to them. It's a very warm and cozy feeling to know that you're accepted and supported, especially with all the alienation and rejection that the J6 defendants have experienced. They have a place to fit in, a place to share and not feel judged. The only way to continue this work is for more to join forces with us and assist in aiding the many January 6 defendants and their families.

Recently I was having a conversation with a J6 wife, and she said she was lonely and sad, that her husband is about to go to prison and her kids are away at school; the life that she once knew has completely changed. She, as well as many others, keeps asking, "What happens now?" and is looking for hope. Hope is something missing from the lives of those living in this nightmare. You have these men and women coming out of prison, and when they do, they will need a lot of support. They will have to rebuild their lives, look for gainful employment, and start over.

They will need financial assistance. Some will need a new place to live, some will need means of travel, and the list is long. In addition, the need for mental health support and mentorship will be vital to rebuilding. We must provide as much community to these families as possible and put a cushion underneath to soften this blow. They need us to say, "We know this is painful and it hurts really bad, but here is this community that is here to help and support you, and that community will stay until your family is intact again." The connections being made because of this foundation are key to the adjustment of everyone's "new normal" now, and that is one of the main priorities here at Patriot Freedom Project.

Our goal moving forward is to build a profound legal defense fund with a great coalition of lawyers. We aspire to be a resource of information for legal precedent, where there will be access to stark contrasts in prior legal proceedings. We will continue growing our mental health community and providing as many support services to the January 6 defendants and their families as possible. More volunteers, mental health professionals, and employers from all states that want to employ these men and women upon their release are crucial in helping these families get back on their feet.

Be on the lookout, as Patriot Freedom Project will be putting together future events to give a platform for January

6 defendants and their families to tell their stories to the public, with no edits or changes from the media. We also have a docuseries coming out in 2023 that will allow the American people to hear the true, uncut stories and the horror they are living through directly from some J6 families. Our docuseries will highlight for you some of the most heartbreaking of stories and let you hear for yourselves what is truly happening to these people and how harshly their lives have changed.

We still need support here at PFP to continue to help this community. We are in need of financial support to assist families with legal fees, essential needs for the women and children as they live off one income, and commissary needs for the detainees. Many trials will be underway in 2023, and with this DOJ continuing the arrest of Trump supporters, the needs of January 6 defendants and their lawyers are unfortunately anticipated to grow. With continued support of the project and help in spreading the word about the good deeds of PFP, we will be able to assist as many families as possible. But we cannot do it without YOU.

Please visit us at www.patriotfreedomproject.com today to see all the ways you can help support the families, the J6ers, and our efforts in supporting the community.

Thank you for your support and patriotism.

ACKNOWLEDGMENTS

Where to begin? When I set out on this journey, I never imagined it would turn into what it has. The connections I have formed have been life-changing, and I am so humbled by those whose paths I have crossed. There is no greater feeling than the one you experience when you have been able to renew someone's hope; by renewing someone's hope, we are also renewed. This feeling is beyond humbling. I am so grateful to be doing this work, God's work. It was a calling I felt, like a call to duty for God and country. I followed my heart to touch as many other hearts as possible. On this journey, I have had the honor of meeting so many incredible people, and as much as I wish I could mention them all, there are simply too many to list. Please know that I am grateful to each and every one of you that has supported our efforts, and even more grateful for the support of the January 6 defendants and their families.

What I have seen and heard over these past twenty-one months is nothing short of a humanitarian crisis. I have listened to many of these wives, these women, and the desperation and cries for relief at all hours of the day and night when they felt and feel nothing but despair when they couldn't see a way out. But they knew they had a place to run to because of this incredible community I have worked so hard to create for and with so many of these incredible families. It is so sad to listen to these cries for relief and help. I want to make this better for these families. I want these young children to know their dads will be OK and their families will be intact once again. We need to make sure these young children know the police are not bad and that they will always be able to turn to them for help.

My wonderful father was a juvenile detective for many years in the little Jersey Shore town I grew up in. He was always helping in our community. Always bringing kids who came from troubled lives home to our house. My mother would take these kids in and give them so much love. She taught my brother and me that DNA means nothing and LOVE means everything. I learned very early on from my amazing parents that we have to lend our hand to those in need and always pay it forward. I also learned to survive because of the very painful divorce my parents had. Everything changed in my life after they split up, and I had to learn very quickly how to cope. So I took those things I learned from and because of my parents and shared them in the PFP community so others can learn to cope too. This has been a very humbling experience, and I must acknowledge those very close to my heart who lent a helping hand to the Patriot Freedom Project community. A simple thank-you would never be enough.

My Lord and Savior, thank you for trusting me with this task. I am always ready and able to do your work.

Fr. Dan, your kindness, prayers, and teachings have led me to this moment; the moment of giving, being selfless, seeing God in all things, helping those in need, and listening to God when he seeks our attention. You reminded me of the importance of putting God first in our lives, and the significance of the Holy Trinity. Thank you for being so selfless and for helping me through a very hard and difficult time in my life; you taught me how to carry my cross in this life. Thank you for showing up for my family when we needed God's word the most. You are an extraordinary priest, and the Good Lord knew exactly how profound your presence would be in so many lives. God bless you, always.

Ed Martin, you have become an amazing friend and mentor. I am extremely grateful to God that our paths have crossed. You've taught me so much, and I hope I continue to keep hitting those singles! Ed, you are an incredibly selfless person who has the biggest and kindest heart. Thank you for always showing up, not just for me but for all those you have extended your hand to. You're never getting rid of me now, Ed! You are so valued, but please don't ask me to eat any more soup!

Rachel "Rockstar" Semmel. I am so grateful for your friendship and mentorship. Your heart is bigger than this universe, Rachel, and I can never thank you enough for always showing up when I've needed guidance and feedback. You were there when "the COVID" got me; thank the Good Lord you were. You took care of so many of those that are near and dear to my heart when I couldn't during a very hard holiday season for so many. You are such a ray of sunshine and have lightened the load of so many. Thank you so much for being on this journey with me. I love you!

G, a.k.a. "the G-Unit," you came into my life at exactly the right time. What would I have done without you? You have made all the areas of my life better, and for that I am so grateful to and for you. You are going to do amazing things in this world, and I am so humbled I have a front-row seat to see this wonderful show. Thank you, G, for always having my back and straightening out the kinks. I absolutely adore you and love you so much.

JoJo, thank you for fighting for Patriot Freedom Project since the first day we met, and for making sure we were seen and heard. Your tenacity and energy are truly amazing, and you are a force to be reckoned with. Your help and dedication are greatly appreciated and very much needed. You are a loyal and committed person, and I am thankful for your support and friendship. You are doing amazing work, and so many need your skills. I love your dad!

Debbie and Dinesh D'Souza, thank you for showing up when nobody else did. You took a chance on me, and I am honored you did. Your trust means the world to me, and I will never let you down! I could never thank you enough for your concern and generosity to the January 6 wives and children; you single-handedly saved Christmas of 2021 for so many children and did it again in 2022. You are both such amazing humans. May God always bless you both.

Steve Bannon (my fav 😊). Thank you, *War Room*, for giving Patriot Freedom Project a place to advocate for the J6 community and to share the many heartbreaking stories of all the people in need. Mr. Bannon, because of your support and assistance we were able to make a profound impact on the lives of these families and the lawyers too. So many families have been able to keep their heads above water because of the generosity of your loyal supporters. They are what makes America so great. I am forever grateful to you, Steve;

thank you.

Dr. Gorka, you are one of the few who showed up and asked, "What can I do?" I am so appreciative of your support and the hospitality you showed my husband and me on that first visit. Thank you for taking the time to listen and learn what I was able to share with you and for following up when you said you would, to check in on these women and their children. These families are in need of so much help and support; we need more like you, Dr. Gorka. Thank you for your powerful voice and continued support.

Lee Smith, what an incredible and authentic person you are. You have been such a help in this fight. This work requires support and help from so many. We all have a vital role in this somewhere, and you have been so key in this. Thank you so very much for allowing me to come on your show and helping me to share with your listeners the heartache we are witnessing with so many of these families. I appreciate the time you have taken to support the efforts of PFP; I am truly so grateful.

Sean Morgan, you have become such a great friend, a genuinely great friend! You are always there when I need assistance. I could not have finished this book without you. I am forever grateful for your friendship. I am learning so much from you. Thank you for your kindness and for your support. I am so excited to be working with you on the many incredible things that lie ahead. Together, we will bring much-needed help and support to many wives and children who are the true collateral damage of January 6. I know together we will continue the much-needed support as these families deal with a two-tiered justice system. Thank you for being in my corner.

Nick Smith, you are not only the greatest lawyer, but you have become a great friend, and I am truly grateful for your friendship. Thank you for saving Tim from a long prison term when he did nothing wrong. For fighting and defending Tim when it was hard to do. Your support means the world to me and Tim.

Joseph McBride, my brother from another mother. Thank you for your friendship, support, and endorsement of our hard work. Thank you for our great talks. Some days when I am about to call you to "bleep" about something I hear you in my head saying, "Cynthia, Cynthia…," with that Brooklyn accent. I appreciate the time you take to work with me on this project; I am forever grateful.

Alex Brusewitz—you were a supporter very early on. I know the J6 families are very grateful for your support; I know how much I am. I have learned a lot from our conversations. I cannot thank you enough for your wisdom, suggestions, and feedback. Thank you for sharing my vision and producing the documentary with me to tell the heartbreaking stories of these families when nobody else would. Anyone working with you is truly very blessed. Thank you, Alex!

Danny and Austin, thank you for helping me support and tell the many heartbreaking stories that must be told by and for these families. I appreciate your support and your help so much. Thank you for being so kind to the children and lifting their spirits. You are both truly amazing humans, and I really adore you both so much. I am looking forward to the great things that lie ahead.

To all the fearless lawyers who have stepped up to the front lines and have shown what a backbone looks like. Thank you for defending our God-given constitutional rights. Your hard work and your time away from your families are beyond appreciated. It has been an honor to get to know so many of you. Your support of this project means the world not only to me but to the many families you are fighting for. *May God always bless and keep you and your families.*

ABOUT THE AUTHOR

Cynthia Hughes is a New Jersey mother, wife, and founder of a nonprofit organization called Patriot Freedom Project. Her efforts to support the January 6 community have not gone unnoticed; she's gained the support of influential figures such as President Donald Trump, Dinesh D'Souza, Steve Bannon, Dr. Sebastian Gorka, and many more.

 Cynthia's strength stems not only from her connection with God but also from her connection to the wives and children of those who are enduring political imprisonment in America. It's through this connection and sense of community that she has been able to raise over one million dollars and help countless families receive financial, emotional, and religious assistance.

Made in the USA
Coppell, TX
08 March 2023

13962136R00079